12/1/17

Dear Char[...]

Start each
day with
thank you in
your heart!

Love

Elen[...]

Spread Thanks

Create Miracles Through the Power of Ink

ELENA ANGUITA

BALBOA
PRESS

A DIVISION OF HAY HOUSE

While the content and stories in this book are based on the author's own life experiences, some names and identifying details have been changed to protect the privacy of individuals.

Balboa Press books may be ordered through booksellers or by contacting:

Balboa Press
A Division of Hay House
1663 Liberty Drive
Bloomington, IN 47403
www.balboapress.com
1 (877) 407-4847

Because of the dynamic nature of the Internet, any web addresses or links contained in this book may have changed since publication and may no longer be valid. The views expressed in this work are solely those of the author and do not necessarily reflect the views of the publisher, and the publisher hereby disclaims any responsibility for them.

The author of this book does not dispense medical advice or prescribe the use of any technique as a form of treatment for physical, emotional, or medical problems without the advice of a physician, either directly or indirectly. The intent of the author is only to offer information of a general nature to help you in your quest for emotional and spiritual well-being. In the event you use any of the information in this book for yourself, which is your constitutional right, the author and the publisher assume no responsibility for your actions.

Print information available on the last page.

ISBN: 978-1-5043-8881-8 (sc)
ISBN: 978-1-5043-8882-5 (hc)
ISBN: 978-1-5043-8880-1 (e)

Library of Congress Control Number: 2017914614

Balboa Press rev. date: 10/30/2017

In Praise Of ... *Spread Thanks*

"**S**ending thank you notes is a brilliant way to transform your world. It worked for me in such a miraculous manner! My life and my business have blossomed in ways I could not have even imagined. Thank you, Elena, for the inspiration and showing the world how to *Spread Thanks*." - **Kathi Whitney Davis**, Owner, Over The Moon, Unique Gifts, Scranton, PA.

"While I love my virtual world, I also adore the hands-on connections I can make through handwritten thank you notes. You never know the ripple effects that you can set in motion through such a simple act of kindness. I would encourage everyone to send a note today and see what happens!" - **Stephanie Veraghen**, Online Consultant and Brand Strategist, Stephanie Veraghen, Inc., Central Florida.

"When I embarked on the process of writing a thank you a day, I found the first week was fun and easy. What happened the second week, though, stunned me! Things showed up in my life that had never shown up before, such as a neighbor leaving fresh tomatoes from their harvest, my writing being published by a widely-read online journal, and my being honored by a friend who asked me to support her. My life has been greatly enriched and I have become a true believer in the power of spreading thanks." - **Anella Wetter**, M.Ed., Writer & Relationship Coach, Lexington, KY

This book is dedicated to my nieces and nephews: Michelle, Derek, Kelly, Mary, and David, whose adorable thank you notes I fell in love with way back when. Little did I know they would change my life.

Contents

Chapter

A Wandering Soul Gets a Big Whoosh

Living in Rome as a young girl, I was surrounded by historical treasures, beautiful scenery, and deep faith, but within my own family I didn't feel that beauty and peace. Instead there was a hopelessness that seemed to permeate our home and I felt it from my earliest awareness.

Even before I started school, I understood that our family was different and my mother was living in a perpetual state of sadness and grief. Shortly after my birth, which was in Spain, my father died leaving my mother to raise us three small girls all by herself. She couldn't understand why her God had abandoned her by taking her husband far too soon.

My mother was not from Spain so there was nothing but tragic memories there for her. She was in fact an intrepid American living abroad, so she decided to relocate our little family to her favorite city in all the world: *Rome, Italy.* As a young widow with three babies in tow, this was a pretty gutsy move, but then again, she was a very

1

special woman. She chose to raise us in the Roman Catholic Church (even though her *own faith* was shaken) for us to be exposed to faith. But no matter what she did, she could not shake off her loneliness and despair. It was while she was in Italy that she started to wrestle with a few personal demons, namely depression and alcoholism, which persisted for most of her life.

When the beauty and tranquility of Rome could not save her, she gave up on Italy and decided to return home to America with us, while she searched for herself and a way to regain her health and strength. I had just become a teenager so this was a massive adventure for me. My stomach was in knots as the plane touched down on American soil. And where did we take up residence you may ask? Under the bright lights of New York? Enjoying the majesty of the Rocky Mountains? *No.* We went to the place my grandmother resided, my mother's hometown of Scranton, Pennsylvania.

Open to the Possibilities

Talk about culture shock. The Colosseum in Rome one day, and coal mines the next. I was bewildered and excited with all the new experiences, but I did know one thing for certain: I had to be strong for my mother and be a good girl. So I assimilated and studied and tried to make friends. I was the model of a responsible daughter. But deep inside, I was still seeking my own place in the world, my own purpose which I knew had to be more than mastering mathematics, making meals, and saying my prayers.

I distinctly remember both the wonderment and the challenges of adjusting to our new lives. It was the same time that my own spiritual awakening was happening. I've been on a spiritual journey of my own since turning 13, open to the many possibilities the world had to offer.

I used to think that "big awakenings" would strike someone like a bolt of lightning, but for me, my perspective opened up quite organically. Even as a teenager, I would ask the big questions like, "What is my mission?" and, "There has to be a purpose to all this." And I followed my mother's path, gradually turning away from the strict dogma of the Catholic religion, as I began searching for my own answers.

On that path, however, I still accepted that life was about *being good* and *doing good*. Deep in my bones, I knew I would find a way to improve the human condition and make the world a better place. I've just kind of always known that, but who could have foreseen it would take another 40 years to really discover *how* to do it? But when I did, it was not long before I started to vibrate at a whole new level and I felt myself and my whole world transform. This book is about that energy shift and how simple --- *yet mind-blowing* --- it can be.

Along the way, like many of you perhaps, I found the most incredible books in the process. *Conversations with God* by Neale Donald Walsch was a life-changer for me because it gave me a bigger picture than I could have possibly imagined. And books like *A New Earth* by Eckhart Tolle stirred something deep inside and I kept seeking with a renewed hunger for my own *transformational moment*.

Growing Up in a Hurry

I never lost the wandering soul that I inherited from my mother. I kept searching most of my adult life, until a few years ago. And on that path, I encountered my own share of life's challenges, as we all have. Later in my life, when I worked in corporate, I came to call these challenges AFGEs (pronounced af-ghee – which is an acronym that stands for Another *Freaking* Growth Experience). It's when something messes up royally in your work or in your life, and you try to find a silver lining or some bigger meaning for it.

Feel free to use this term – we all have AFGEs! My first big AFGE came when I was really young and I suddenly realized that I had to grow up in a hurry. One day I was a carefree young school girl playing with friends, exploring the sandy beaches near our home in Ostia, outside of Rome, Italy. The next thing I knew, I woke up at age 13, living in a completely new country and culture, and having to care not only for myself but also the house and my mother. So many days, my mother was in such pain due to depression that she could not make meals, tidy up, or care for our needs.

Not surprisingly, this became a pattern in my life: always being the good girl, the caretaker, not rocking the boat. But in my heart I knew I was destined for something *more*. I just needed to be patient and my "aha" moment would miraculously appear.

So it did. It appeared, and yes, it was when I least expected it and in the last place I might have thought to look. In fact, it had to hit me twice before I really noticed it, before I realized that this might be "the thing" that I'd been waiting for.

But now for the bad news. Like so many transformational moments here on earth, mine was preceded by a colossal amount of personal and professional chaos (yes, a whole pile of AFGEs) happening in what was otherwise a pretty organized and predictable adult life up to that point. If you are currently in chaos, where you have keep dodging more crap or another "growth experience," then take heart. I suspect that you're likely just in the eye of the storm yourself, like I was, and when it clears, you too will be at peace, and moving forward with a vastly improved outlook. What a great system, right?

Facing Storms at Work

So yes, let me tell you about the *storm* before the *calm*. Here's what was going on. I'll just relate the highlights, and then we can get on to the *solution*.

A few years before my "aha" moment, I was just coming out of a severe situation, where I had been working for a new company, doing high level sales for them and with great success, when suddenly they refused to pay my commissions. I was by myself at that time, not in a relationship so I had no one for moral or financial support. But it was a lot of money I was owed and I really needed it to live. I felt strongly that I should stand up for myself and even sue the company, if necessary.

In reality, it was a David and Goliath kind of experience because the company had deep pockets and the "Executives" were determined not to give me what I had earned. I later discovered that the practice of non-payment was quite common in this company. At the point that one account grew very large, it would arbitrarily be designated as a *house-account* and the salesperson would be cut off from getting any further commissions.

But at the time, I thought I was the only person in this situation. "Wow. How could this possibly be happening?" I thought. Since I was typically positive in my daily outlook, this blow made me feel depressed and burnt out. For the first time in my life, I got to experience what my mother had struggled with for all those years, and it made me much more sympathetic for what she had been through.

My business associates and friends from other companies told me, "Elena, stuff like this happens all the time in sales. Companies refuse to pay salespeople. You just have to move on." Even my own brother-in-law, whose opinion I respect, gave me that very same advice. Yet, at the end of the day, I just couldn't let it go. A little voice in me said, "Yes, perhaps this happens all the time, but I need to stand up for myself, win, lose or draw!" It wasn't so much that I was going up against the big guys just for myself, but I felt I needed to stand up for others, helping other employees so this wouldn't happen to anyone else.

It was my decision. I stayed strong, hired a lawyer, sued the company, and sweated it out. Come what may, this was something I just felt compelled to do. It was a nasty fight at times and there were more cloudy days than sunshine during that period. Long story short, by the time a settlement was reached and the lawyers got their cut, it was not a financial windfall. But importantly to me, it was a moral victory and a pivotal moment in my life. I may have been alone but I was not going to be a victim ever again.

Was the Chaos Finally Over?

I wish I could say life settled down and got back to normal, but it didn't. I felt vindicated and found a new job, but just as I got established again, I found myself in the middle of another dark period. I was facing the eminent death of a man I had come to care for. I remember helping him during the middle of that illness, when a first quiet *whoosh* came over me, a surge of energy that flowed over me and through me with such a reassuring warmth. Within that emotion, I could feel an idea whispering to me: *a thank you a day.*

But when that first *whoosh* happened, I didn't act on it because my life was back to chaos and upheaval again. My long-awaited "aha" moment would have to wait just a little longer while I struggled just to get from one day to the next, moment by moment, breath by breath.

The man I had been dating, himself a gifted healer, ironically enough, was dying of cancer. I did what I could for him, dealing with the anger and the pain, the messy bits muddled in amongst the more mundane days, and I listened to him negotiate with God for a reprieve. But it was not to be. I kept a vigil right through to his final acceptance that death was here and it was time to go. It was an honor to have been chosen to help him transition to death, but after months of supporting him through his marathon, I was exhausted in all possible ways: mentally, emotionally, physically, and spiritually. Yes, another AFGE. And this one was *big*.

That was 2013. Afterward, I packed up his life, made all the arrangements, did what needed to be done, ever the dutiful servant. Looking back now, it's a bit of a blur really, and I didn't even remember that first *whoosh* until it hit again in 2014. The second time it was louder and much more insistent. The vision clearly was: *"send a thank you a day."*

So the Universe wanted me to write and send a thank you note every day? It sounded a bit odd, but the feeling kept bubbling up inside me, and I started doing it. I told myself, "Let me get some thank you notes. I'll start writing them and see what happens." And so the journey began. I had no idea where it would take me but felt an urgency to embark on it, nonetheless.

Welcoming Goodness and Light

After maybe just a week or two, I started seeing pleasant serendipities, small things at first. I would be driving and notice the traffic in my direction was smooth sailing while the other side of the highway was bumper-to-bumper. I said, "Thank goodness I'm on this side." The next day, I would find just the perfect parking spot in front of the place I needed to be, just in the nick of time. The day after, a dear old friend would call me just when I was thinking that I would like to reconnect with her but I had lost her number.

When I thought about the timing and began seeing a pattern, I began to question, "Could it be my daily written notes of gratitude were actually *the catalyst* for so many nice things happening with such consistency?" So I said to myself, I should begin to take note and see if it does happen every single day. And yes, it was occurring *every single day*. I thought, I have to really start recording these wonderful serendipities at the end of each day, so I don't forget them, and I did that too. It took only a few minutes a day but it was transforming me and everything around me.

This whole practice was just giving me such a boost that I couldn't imagine my day without it. My mental health and physical body felt wonderful and balanced. I hardly ever got a cold. Work seemed surprisingly effortless and there were always daily surprises that made me giggle, I felt like the carefree young girl I was so many years ago growing up in Rome.

Within a few months of sending a written thank you note each day, my energy level was so much better. I started to vibrate with the knowledge that the positive results were consistent, and more often than not, I was experiencing things that were nothing short of miraculous on a daily basis. That's when I knew that I was onto something and it was something *big*.

A Movement for the Masses

What an exciting thought --- *If I could do this, surely anyone could?* It's so simple and I can describe how it works, explain the power of the practice, while giving examples and inspirational stories to keep each new person motivated. The more I thought about it, I realized, this is what I have been called to do. *Spread thanks*. Determined to keep up with my daily practice, which was now entering its second year, I made a promise to myself. I'm going to write all this down and share it with the world. I'll reach people who are exhausted, discouraged with life, beaten down and depressed, and asking themselves, *"Is this all there is?"*

Because now I know with certainty that there is so much more to the world than what we see. We can impact our internal energy and our external circumstances with gratitude. I can prove it. I have proven it and as more people try it and feel its power, I can see the world transforming exponentially.

Imagine the emotional *whoosh* to the person who gets one of your daily thank you notes? Completely out of the blue, they feel a tangible pat on the back for something nice they did, and it boosts their self-esteem and energy. They pay it forward, responding with kindness to their circle of influence, and before long, we've got so much more than merely *mail* --- we've got masses of people creating daily miracles for themselves and others.

Starting Out with Simplicity in Mind

So in the beginning, I made it a habit to write my notes in the morning before starting my day. The first couple of notes were really fun to write. I could easily think of someone to thank, such as a friend who helped me out with something, and I found myself putting pen to paper with great enthusiasm. I hadn't told anyone about my new experiment and I was eager to hear my friend's reactions (if any) to receiving an unexpected handwritten thank you note in the mail. Looking back now, I call this my honeymoon period, since it was so full of joy and excitement.

However, within a week or two, I ran out of obvious friends to thank and I hit a dry period. I would sit at the table and, for the first time in my life, I could not remember a single person who made my life easier the day before, no one to be the recipient of my daily thank you note. *Crap!* I needed to rethink this and get better at noticing what was going on around me. Surely someone must have been nice to me yesterday, right? I didn't want this whole "thank you note a day" idea to become any kind of chore so I resolved to pay more attention in the future.

Sure enough, once I starting staying more focused, even while doing mundane daily activities, I found all sorts of kindnesses going on. Even when I would be filling my car with gas, checking into a hotel, meeting new clients, or shopping for groceries, I found myself noticing that there were little helpers along the way. They made me smile or showed special care that they didn't have to do. I made it a game to find the "recipient" of my next thank you note and it became fun again. My mood was lifted and I was more determined than ever to keep on going with my "thank you note a day" and see if I could truly change the world.

Now it is your turn to join in and I hope you will. Collectively, we have tremendous power. As I walk you through the stories of transformation and wonder in my own gratitude journey, I urge you to start your own practice, to sit and write a simple thank you note a day. In each chapter, I'll offer a few tips and techniques to keep you moving forward, overcome hurdles and keep you smiling, plus I'm happy to end each chapter with a sample thank you note so you can see how easy this really is to do. Have you got your pen ready? OK. Let's go.

How to Spread Thanks: Time to Get Started

The first bit of advice I love to share is not to be critical of yourself in any way. Nothing has to be perfect with your notes, you just have to do one a day. Sit down with your pen, write a little card or note, and send it to someone in thanks. Anyone can do that.

I just started with some notes I had in my house, so you can do that too. Or stop by the store on your way home and pick up a cute little box to get you started. Choose a design that makes you smile, so you'll feel good when you sit down to write your first few notes. Pick up a package of stamps to have them on hand; then you won't have any reason not to follow through.

Even if you miss a day as your begin the practice, don't be discouraged. Of course, we're all busy and sometimes time will slip away despite our best intentions. If that happens, just pick yourself back up, shake yourself off, and say, "It's worth it. I can do this. It *will* make a difference."

Like any habit, be aware that it can take consistent effort for 20 or 30 days in a row to really make it part of your every day routine, but I assure you, it's a practice that is well worth doing. When you share thanks, it boosts your mood, it raises the self-esteem of the person who gets the card, and it reminds everyone that there is so much good in this world, more than we could ever measure.

Here are a few quick ideas to get you through those first few weeks. Send a note to your neighbor and drop it in their box or under their door on your way out to work; maybe they helped collect your mail or walk your dog at some recent point, or offered to run an errand for you when your car was in the shop. Let them know how much you appreciated that, even if it was last month. It will still be meaningful to them.

Or you could thank your spouse, partner, child or co-worker for taking care of something important for you when you were completely stressed. When you send someone close to you a note, they will begin to understand your daily practice and encourage you to keep it going. Maybe they might even join in and start their own daily routine which incorporates gratitude. It's that simple to get started. What do you have to lose?

A Notable Note of Thanks: Thank You for Being a Friend

One of the first thank you notes that I remember sending was to my friend, Kathi, who helped me spruce up my place. I've never been very comfortable with *change* anyway, and I was not very confident when it came to choosing accessories or coordinating colors. But I knew my friend Kathi had a knack for this kind of thing. I was so happy when she came over and helped me change what was a formal and traditional looking living space into something that was so much more in keeping with my personality.

She chose warm sunset colors that I just love and was so creative, I was in awe of what she could do. I thanked her in person of course, several times, but I thought, what if I write her a note? That might be special. As I wrote it, I began to feel the joy and excitement I did when she first transformed the space, and I hoped that she would feel a spillover of the joy she gave to me, when she got the note. That's exactly what happened. She said she felt special and appreciated and thanked me for my *thank you*. It was a simple act for me but it meant a lot to her. Here's what I wrote.

Dear Kathi:

Thank you for all your wonderful decorating ideas. Who knew that a fresh coat of paint and a few new pillows could transform the look and feel of my living room! I just love my new space. What a gift you gave me and what a gift you are to all your friends!

Love,

Elena

Chapter

Putting Pen to Paper

It was just an ordinary day and I was clearing out my bedroom closets, when I looked down and my heart caught in my throat. I saw my mother's handwriting peeking out from under a stack of photographs and greeting cards from years gone by. I recognized her handwriting immediately. I could hardly believe it had been 10 years since she had passed away, so I was even more in awe of finding this treasure.

As I gently picked up the first card, I noticed several more from her underneath, and I wistfully decided to read each one that morning, despite the pangs of longing for her that I still felt in my heart. As I opened the first card, I could see it was a humorous one that she had sent me to congratulate me after ending a terrible job. As I read her funny note, in her unmistakable handwriting, I was instantly transported in time to the event that triggered the card. It felt like *forever* ago. I chuckled at her words and was reminded of her wit, bone-dry and somewhat sarcastic but, oh so sharp! How thoughtful of Mom to send me a card, and how like her to make a joke of it, in such a time of crisis. I loved that about her.

I smiled and eagerly opened the next one, which was a birthday card in which she had simply written, "Much love, Mom". Again I felt transported back in time and I felt her presence, her love, and her support. I continued the exercise of opening and reading her cards, thoroughly enjoying the experience of traveling through time and feeling her with me again.

Then I came upon the last card, one she had written during her illness, and I noticed the stark difference in her handwriting, which was weak and especially hard to decipher. My eyes welled with tears as I felt a flood of emotions wash over me, this time recalling the dark days that passed from the time she was first diagnosed with lung cancer, to the chemo and radiation treatments, and her eventual death. I closed the last card and gently wept. It was quite the unexpected journey.

After a few minutes, I returned to my task, and that's when my eyes caught sight of my grandmother's writing. I called her Nana and just glancing at the envelope, her image sprung to mind immediately. My Nana was a petite woman, barely 4' 11" tall, but with stately elegance and impeccable taste. She would walk into a room, shoulders high, in her matching outfit, stiletto heels, and gloves (of course) and people would stop and watch her. To me, Nana was, and always will be, the most elegant and loving woman I ever knew.

As I began reading her letter, I realized she'd sent it to me when I first went away for job training with IBM. As I felt her presence, a whole new set of memories came to mind. I remembered it was Nana who got the house ready for us when we needed to move back to America. It was she who would cook extraordinary holiday meals and she who made the best fudge known to man. But most especially, as I was reading her letter, I felt her loving energy, which was so patient, so sweet, so fabulous, and could only come from *My One and Only Nana*.

Eventually I made my way through the papers and cards, and near the end of the process, I found a card from my niece Kelly. It was a thank you note she had written when she was 11 or 12, thanking me, her "Aunt Elena", for a birthday present. From the handwriting, I could tell Kelly was not yet in high school and sure enough, just from holding her card in my hand, I could see her in my mind's eye at that age, full of energy and enthusiasm, such an affectionate child.

Kelly was one who was always eager for hugs and saying, "I love you." Face beaming with a great smile, she would always see a glass as being half full. I felt a smile on my face recalling the famous Kelly story when she was learning to ride a bike and fell hard on the gravel road. She got up right away and looked at her Dad. Rather than bursting into tears, she exclaimed, "Daddy, daddy, did you see how *far* I went?"

As I closed Kelly's card and tucked it back away with the others, I was amazed at the evocative power of handwriting. I was literally transported in time with each note I read and I felt the presence of those special people, conveying their essence and their state of mind just from the mere appearance of their words on those pages.

There was something very special not only about the notes but about the *handwriting* itself. Could I have stumbled upon something?

The Power of the Pen

What a powerful lesson I had that day while doing just a mundane task like cleaning out the closet. I discovered first-hand the power of the handwritten word and that is why handwriting became such an intrinsic part of my gratitude practice. I totally feel that the key to success with the practice of sending a card a day is because they are handwritten inside and out.

I just don't think that the same emotion and energy comes across when you send a thank you note that is typed out on a keyboard, rather than handwritten. And although I'm sure you said a personal thank you out loud in the moment that you were helped, there is still tremendous value on a number of levels for following up with a handwritten thank you note. It is a tangible, touchable, and unique form of thank you that only you can create. It will thrill the person getting it, to realize they have been valued for their thoughtfulness and give them a boost to their mood and their self-esteem.

The truth is that in our busy world, too often we just mumble a thank you and rush off because we have to get to our next appointment or get home and, in that preoccupied moment, the thank you that you gave might not have been as heartfelt or even heard, since the next client would be stepping up to be served.

While you may think your handwriting is messy, you can still do this practice. You can take a bit more care with the note than you might for a grocery list, and the recipient will still appreciate your effort even if your writing isn't perfect.

I found it interesting when I looked up the value of handwriting, the science behind it I mean, I was reminded that the ability to read and write is key to lifelong success in this world. Literacy begins the moment a child picks up his or her first pencil or crayon, as it did for you. The truth is that the connection between learning handwriting skills and success in reading has existed for many years in education, and I feel that it is crucially important today that we not lose sight of this. Research shows that the physical act of writing, first phonetically, then with accurate spelling, creates a bridge to literacy (the ability to read) at a very early age. Youngsters who learned to print and then write were better readers in fluency, comprehension, and other language arts components.

So yes, I love handwriting. I admit it. But why would this powerful connection exist between writing and literacy? Even in this world where computers and phones seem to be everywhere at every age, I still believe that the pen is mightier than the keyboard. It certainly is when it comes to sending thank you notes, that's for sure. It's more personal and unique. It conveys a high level of personal attention that someone took, just to say thanks to you.

When I researched further I found all kinds of benefits that handwriting brings to our lives. While it might just seem to be a quaint tradition that is long since passed, it's not. Handwriting actually activates a unique neural circuit that makes learning easier, and engages more parts of your brain than keyboarding does. Handwriting involves movement because you hold the pen and touch the paper to create letters, directing movement through your thoughts. When the ink hits the page, it becomes a personalized representation of ourselves. Even in this fast-paced world today, we write reminders to ourselves, notes, letters, cards, and we sign our name on checks and legal documents to prove our identity and agreement.

Operating a keyboard just doesn't have this level of engagement with your brain; all you have to do is hit the right keys. There simply isn't the same intimacy when a note is sent by keyboard or printed out in laser text and sent that way. That's why I felt the impression of my loved ones years after they had written those cards to me. Even after their death, the emotion remains because those cards and envelopes were written by their own hand.

Real Addressed Mail is Exciting

Another thing to remember is that real mail is so rare that it makes your card even more special to the recipient. Think about it. What do you get in the mail these days? Nothing very positive I expect; mine is made up almost entirely of bills, solicitations, advertisements, and other junk mail. Then lo and behold, there is a hand-written thank you note to cut through the negativity, and deliver with it joy, kindness, generosity, and love. Thank you notes are by far my favorite piece of mail.

For years while my nieces and nephews were growing up, I would relish the thank you notes I received. How adorable, each with a distinct "personality" of the writer, with a distinct handwriting style. Those thank you notes would literally buoy my spirit, change my attitude, and grace my day with joy. And that is precisely what your note will do. Can you imagine impacting 365 people in this way every year, through a relatively simple habit?

I trust that I have made the case as to why there is something so special about the handwritten thank you note. Not only does it take longer to compose than a text or email (which, in turn, helps elevate your energy as the writer) but it creates an individualized expression for you to send. Your handwriting is unique to you, which personalizes the communication that much more.

The recipient may recognize your handwriting and instantly feel joyous to have received a note from you, as a friend or a dear acquaintance. But then imagine the stranger you may have only met once. The note from you will be powerful because they know you cared enough about them to take that extra step, pick up your pen, use their name, and send it with a stamp. What a significant transfer of energy! What a gift. That's why I love this practice of handwritten thank you notes; there is hardly anything more special to receive.

Tips to Spread Thanks: Finding People to Thank

The recipient of your daily thank you note can be anyone in your life, and you can draw from an infinite pool of people. It can go to a person whom you see each day or be someone you will never see again. Many of my recipients are service providers because I travel a lot with my job and stay at many hotels, but I have also sent notes to relatives, friends, neighbors, teachers, and mentors.

If you are running out of ideas of whom to thank next, here are some of my best suggestions for categories of people you can send a card of thanks to. And at the end of the book, I have written out 20 samples for each of these thank you notes if you need a little more help getting started.

- The client who purchased your services or products.
- The friend or relative who stopped what he or she was doing to listen to your situation and provide support.
- The young person living in the apartment across the hall who helped to troubleshoot and fix your computer issues. Complimenting a young person on a skill they possess can be hugely impactful in boosting their confidence.
- The person conducting a job interview that you attended.
- The police officer who helped when you were stranded on the side of the road with car trouble.
- The friend or relative who helped get your children off the school bus when you were stuck in traffic or running late.
- The store clerk who helped you get a heavy purchase into your car.
- The receptionist who helped you reach the "right" person in the organization.
- The administrative assistant who helped secure the appointment you needed to make with someone hard to get a meeting with.
- The finance clerk or HR officer at the company you work for.

- The concierge at the hotel who secured a dinner reservation at a "hot" restaurant for you to impress your client, date, or spouse.
- The housekeeper at the hotel where you just stayed.
- The teacher who spent time with your child outside of the school day to make sure he or she learned a difficult math concept.
- The student who went above and beyond (if you're the teacher).
- The Good Samaritan who helped you change a tire by the side of the road.
- The nurse who made sure your loved one or yourself was comfortable during a hospital visit.
- The doctor who took special care of you (or loved one) by spending extra time to explain the medical condition, the upcoming procedure, and the follow-up care.
- The colleague who worked overtime to help you get your project out the door.
- The massage therapist who erased your stress with magic kneading.
- The handyman or tradesperson who repaired something in your home recently.

Tips to Spread Thanks: How to Write a Good Thank You Note

Getting started is usually a bit difficult for people until they get used to the flow of writing thank you notes. It might be many years since you wrote your last one. If you need some help, here are five of my best writing prompts to get you started on your first notes.

- This note is to thank you for _____
  _____.

- It made me feel so good when you helped me with _____
  _____.

- Please accept my sincere appreciation for your help with __
  _____.

- I still smile when I think of your kindness last week when you
  _____.

- Thank you so much for your time when you helped me __
  _____.

As you create the whole note, try to write three sentences of meaningful content. They don't have to be long. This isn't a literary work of art, you just have to be sincere. We tend to be our own worst critics, so don't let that deter you. Silence that inner critic who might be telling you that your penmanship is sloppy or you're not sufficiently eloquent or whatever. Don't be critical of your handwriting or word choices because they will be good enough, no problem. If you feel really stuck, I like to suggest that you close your eyes, put your hand over your heart, feel the beats, and ask yourself, "What would I like to say from the heart?" Then just let those words flow.

In the beginning, you might like to write a practice note first. If you're unsure of what to say, just write the note on a piece of scrap paper first. Let the words and your feelings flow. Perhaps write a few extra sentences and, once you have a draft, you can go back and read your note aloud or to yourself, to see how it sounds. Then you can choose the best three sentences out of the group, or perhaps you might rephrase a few words in the note. That way you can choose precisely the words you want to express how the person or gesture made you feel.

A Notable Note of Thanks: Finding Gratitude by the Side of the Road

You might wonder when I actually started to feel the transformational power of this practice. The first time I was aware that I was now able to see the good in just about any "bad situation" was when I was driving home from Philadelphia. I was unable to avoid running over two-by-four pieces of lumber that had fallen off a truck a few seconds before.

It made a horrible noise and two tires went flat immediately, forcing me to pull over. As it turned out, I was one of several motorists that day on the side of the road with flat tires, due to the same road debris. I was instantly grateful that the situation had not been worse because I could have collided with another car, for instance. So I waited patiently for emergency road service to arrive.

The tow truck drivers first on the scene towed a fellow stranded motorist and me to the nearest tire center which was a Walmart, and I immediately noticed how willing everyone was to help me. I waited outside for my car to be repaired and noticed how beautiful the weather was. It slowly started to dawn on me that I was happy, grateful, and I actually felt blessed. After all, I was fine, nothing truly serious had occurred on the highway, I was among people willing to help me, and the weather was gorgeous. *Holy Cow.* I actually felt very grateful that it was just a near accident rather than a tragic one.

I made sure to take down the helpful manager's name so I had my thank you note recipient for the next day. I had handled the situation with calm and composure, a good lesson for me, and I was still able to meet my sister and brother-in-law for dinner.

So I chose to see that it wasn't a bad thing, but rather a good thing that had happened to me that day. Could a "bad" thing actually be an opportunity for a lesson? And wouldn't that ultimately be a good thing, not a bad thing? Wow, I had shifted. My perception of the situation was entirely different from what it would've been in the past, and I know this was a product of this special daily practice that I was now getting pretty good at. Here is my note to Mark, the manager of the Walmart Supercenter Automotive department.

Dear Mark:

This is Elena, the "damsel in distress" you helped yesterday. I felt truly stranded when my car unexpectedly hit the debris on the turnpike and blew out two tires! When the tow truck finally came and took me to the nearest tire service location (your Walmart), I was resigned to spend another hour at least waiting for my car to be repaired.

Instead, to my delight, you found the right tires for my car in minutes and had me back on the road in less than half an hour! That has to be a record! I was even able to get home in time for my scheduled dinner with my sister.

Thank you for the excellent service! You turned the adversity into a pleasant anecdote.

Sincerely yours,
Elena

Chapter

Your Daily Routine in 3 Easy Steps

I n October 2014, just a few weeks into the practice of writing and sending my daily thank you notes, I was working from home and got a voice mail message from Susan. She was one of my most loyal clients and she asked me to call her at my earliest opportunity. She was such a loyal client, and she had already renewed the annual license for her school's software program back in July, so I assumed she was simply calling me with a random question about one of the online courses offered by the company.

When I got that call from Susan, my sales figures for the year were marginal. This was not from lack of hard work but because the company had set really aggressive sales expectations and we were all experiencing some unfortunate circumstances, such as school closures. Since my year-to-date sales were so far off from goal, I had resigned myself to not meeting my targets for the year. It was not a good feeling but, nonetheless, I decided to look ahead to the following year and focus on 2015 being much better.

Then the phone rang. "Elena," Susan began, "I know this sounds a little crazy but have you ever had a client ask to renew their account ahead of schedule? We're concerned about potential changes in the school board in November with the upcoming election and I don't want there to be problems with the contract renewal next year."

I could hardly believe my ears! At first I thought she was kidding but she wasn't. I said I would look into it, obviously excited at the prospect of bringing in more revenue for 2014. Susan surprised me again when she asked about renewing multiple years in advance. At that point, my jaw was hanging open. "Sure," I stammered, "what did you have in mind?" "I was thinking of a five-year contract." *Five years?* Wow. That would be a miracle I thought.

I told Susan I would check with management. The second I got off the phone, I immediately called my manager and together we computed the sale over 5 years to yield more than $1.1 million in revenue. He and I were both thrilled and he said that of course it could be worked out.

Goodbye marginal year! Hello stellar sales figures for me for 2014! I was still a bit shocked and almost incredulous when that order, which represented a value of more than $1 million to the company, was closed in about three weeks. I had never done that before and I don't know anyone else who did either. Not only did this bring good fortune to me, but also to my manager who, for the first time since joining the company, was able to meet *his* goal.

It was an absolute stroke of luck … *or was it?*

Could my "stroke of luck" be a result of my daily thank you note practice? I just knew that this was not a coincidence. I had been doing this daily thank you card writing for a few months, and I had been experiencing a number of fun "serendipities", but this was definitely the first mind-blowing coincidence. It actually became the first of many more wonderful "aha!" moments that kept happening with regularity to me. I knew it was directly because I had opened myself up to the power of being thankful and that is what made all the difference.

I began to tell my friends about closing a $1.1 million order, achieving my goal, and helping my team to meet its target. And each person kept saying, "Oh my God, that is a miracle!" So I began calling my daily serendipities or coincidences by a new name: I called them daily miracles because, yes, to me they were *miracles*.

This was truly a pivotal moment for me because it was then that I knew I had to *share* this simple practice with the world. I could not keep it to myself. I felt I had uncovered something so simple, yet so magical and powerful. It was such an easy way to bring good things into one's life which involved three simple steps: the daily practice of paying attention to the day, expressing thanks to people by the way of a handwritten card, and then recording the miracle "aha" moment at the end of the day, because for sure it will happen.

Where is All This Extra Good Coming From?

When I started writing daily thank you notes in September 2014, within just a week or two I began to notice little coincidences showing up on a daily basis. I would hear of a major road construction project just in time for me to avoid that route on my trip. A car would pull out of the "perfect" parking spot just as I was approaching the store and that spot would be mine. I would find just the exact items when shopping and very often they were on sale.

All these "serendipities" made my life just that little bit easier and fun and I enjoyed watching for them. Each time one happened, I whispered a quick *thank you*. If the good thing involved someone else's assistance, I would take notice of their name and put them on my formal thank you list to receive a handwritten card. But many times, it was just good luck coming my way, a series of great things that made my life more joyful, prosperous, and exciting.

At first I thought these were merely strange or coincidental occurrences, but after the fabulous experience with Susan renewing her account, I thought I should actually write these down and keep track of them each day. I wanted to see if they were indeed happening on a consistent basis.

I did this by keeping a little notebook where I could record the details of these extra positive events at the end of the day, and I began calling them my "daily miracles." Not only that, I told other people about it, the link between being grateful and having more and more good fortune, and they agreed that it worked for them too.

However you define it, I can tell you for sure that a miracle will appear every day, once you are in the habit of writing a thank you note a day. It may be small, it may be big, it may be personal, it may be financial, or it may only be meaningful to *you*, but no matter, *it is there.*

I know with certainty these are not serendipities, they're miracles. And once I started looking at the bigger picture, and really starting thinking about this, I realized it's all energy. I believe it starts with the energy of handwriting, because you engage so many parts of your body and mind when you use your pen, as you create and write your thoughts on paper. There's energy you put into that and it counts as a positive vibe out to the world around you, and set the intention that you believe in goodness everywhere, that you believe in love.

Regardless of size, shape or impact, these are all "aha" moments that will increase your energy. Then when you say thank you for those daily miracles, you in turn send waves of good energy, happiness, and love out to the world around you.

Three Steps to a Thank You a Day

You can probably see that while writing and sending the card is the main point of this process, it turns out that there are three steps to making this process into a daily habit and starting to create your own miracles.

Step One is to pay attention, to be mindful and present as you go about your daily routines. Keep your eyes wide open, looking forward, not just trained on your phone. Put a smile on your face, and meet the gaze of those around you. Stay focused on even small tasks and treat everything you do as important. This step engages you in life, and sets you up to find the person whom you will thank with a note later that day or in the morning, depending on your own preference.

Being mindful is now a habit for me and it has enhanced all aspects of my life. Each day starts out positive and continues to get better and better as I stay present and expect the best in myself and others. I haven't had a bad day in months that I can remember. Challenges, yes, we all have them and so do I. Some days clients don't pay their invoices, or my forecast report is late and my manager calls me on it, but it's okay. I try to remain present and look for the good in that situation. Maybe it's all just another one of those AFGEs, a growth experience, and what I do to remedy this particular work situation, I can use again if I need to.

So just to review, here's how this first step works. During the day, pay attention to those around you, and to each event as you're experiencing it. Seek out the subject of your next thank you note and keep an eye out for your daily miracle. Be mindful.

Now you're ready for Step Two, which is to write the actual thank you note. *How?* Again, be in the moment, feel the gratitude, and remember the person who helped you. Close your eyes for a moment and bring yourself to feel that thankfulness. Feel it, even for a few seconds.

Here's how I do it. I never just write the thank you note. I think about it and I try to recall the joy. I feel the gesture the person did for me. I try to relive the feeling of relief when my car was fixed or how I felt when I was reunited with something precious I had lost. Whatever the reason for the note, I want to recreate the feeling so I can add that emotion to my written message. The emotion I feel flows through my hand, then onto the card and it changes my vibrational frequency. I always feel warm and have sense of accomplishment when I complete the writing of my note for the day.

In Step Three, you write an entry in your Daily Miracle journal. Describe the miracle, serendipity, or coincidence (whatever you'd like to call it) that you experienced that day. This can just be a few lines long, not hard to do at all. There will be at least one, I promise. If you find that a daily miracle doesn't come to mind, then try to be more mindful the next day so that you will recognize it when it happens.

Tips to Spread Thanks: How to Recognize a Miracle

When you are present, mindful, and actively practicing gratitude, you will start to see good things happening to you all the time. The trick is to not take things for granted. Everything is occurring for a reason and it is good to be in the right frame of mind to notice it.

As you are going about your day, pay attention to each interaction and each transaction. It could be on the phone or in person, any time that you connect with someone. Make a conscious choice to be present as life unfolds so you don't miss any of the simple gestures of kindness and love. Look the person in the eye who is serving you. Seek to be kind to them regardless of how they may be acting. Notice any time in your day that you feel taken care of or you feel like you are part of something greater than what is obvious, and that could be your daily miracle.

Be aware that your daily miracle does not have to be about the other person. It could be receiving an unexpected card or invitation in the mail. It might be when an appointment opens up because of a cancellation by someone else, and you can get in the door earlier than you expected. Your miracle might be a call from a close friend that made your day. Or you might open a drawer and find a gift card for your favorite store that you forgot you had, or you might find a treasured piece of jewelry that you thought you'd lost. All these things, small or large, can be your daily miracle.

Tips to Spread Thanks: Creative Ways to Catch Someone's Name

When I explain this process of mailing off a note a day, I hear that it is sometimes a struggle to get the person's full name and address in order to thank them with a note, especially if they are working in a service position in a store, hotel or other setting where you might only meet them casually on one occasion.

I advise that you take notice of the person's first name while they are serving you, if you feel this is the thank you note you will be sending for the day. If it's a commercial company, I try to contact the manager by phone as soon after the exemplary service was rendered. You might ask for the manager or supervisor of a specific department if you know how the place is organized, or you can ask to speak to the owner if it is a small enterprise.

Once you reach the individual in charge, explain the purpose of your inquiry by saying that you received special service from the employee and you'd like to show your appreciation by sending a brief note. I find that as long as you are sincere and friendly, the manager will gladly provide the last name and address if you need it. Make sure you spell the names correctly. You might also speak to the Human

Resources or personnel department if you can't reach the manager or owner.

I also find that the Internet is an excellent resource for finding people's names. Company and store websites often have directories with names and phone numbers that are organized by department. Occasionally when leaving a business, if I did not catch the person's name, I will stop and ask the receptionist to help me. They know everyone and if you describe the person who helped you, it's easy enough to get the further details you need from them in order to post a thank you note to the person who assisted you.

Sometimes you forget someone's name that you've been introduced to before or who serves you regularly like someone at the bank or at your hairdresser. Don't be embarrassed if you need to ask again. Just say, "Oh, I'm sorry, I seem to have forgotten your name. I really should know it. What is it again?" They'll say, "It's Michael" and you just say, "Oh, of course, I remember now. Well, thank you, Michael. You were a big help to me today." Then you can follow up as above to seek out the last name and full address.

Notable Note of Thanks: Showing Gratitude for Your Miracles

For this chapter, I am happy to share the note that I wrote to my client Susan, to let her know how her faith in me and our company had such a positive impact when she chose to renew her contract with us in advance for the next five years. As I wrote her this note, I felt the emotion of the great thing she caused to happen and my objective was to convey that emotion to her while still being professional and appropriate in tone. I felt amazing when I dropped this note in the mail because I knew it would make her smile to realize how thankful we all were to her.

November 2014

Dear Susan:

I cannot tell you how much I appreciate your recent order! Having you as a client is just a joy. Not many clients would renew in advance of the due date, let alone request a multi-year contract! What I did not have the chance to tell you was that your order allowed not only me to hit my goal this year but also my entire team! My manager David is simply thrilled, since the goal appeared unattainable this year. That is, until your order came in.

I value your continued support immensely and will have you on the top of my list of reasons to be grateful during this upcoming Thanksgiving holiday.

Best, best wishes,
Elena

Chapter

Saying Thank You Each Day

Some days I really have to dig deep to figure out someone to send my daily thank you note to. It was like that one week while I was traveling with my work throughout Western Pennsylvania. I woke up struggling to think of a recipient for my card that morning. The previous day had been so hectic, I wasn't as present in the moment as I usually try to be, and as I opened my eyes, I couldn't seem to think of an exact person to thank. The day before was just a blur.

I was still enjoying the comfortable bed and the cozy hotel room, and trying not to think about another day of back-to-back appointments, and then I thought, *you know what?* I could write a thank you note to the maid of the hotel where I'm staying.

I remembered that the room had been such a welcome sight when I checked in exhausted the previous evening. I just fell into bed. When I got up to get to my task, I picked up my pen and tried to feel the same gratefulness that I felt the night before when I saw how clean and inviting the room was. Once I held that emotion of gratitude, the words just flowed. It was a simple note.

"Dear Housekeeper: Thank you so much for your hard work. I travel a great deal with my job and I cannot tell you the pleasure of coming back to a clean and inviting hotel room after a long day of meetings or a long trip in the car. I so appreciate you! Sincerely, Elena."

And as I slipped the card into its envelope, I also left a tip which is my usual practice. Just a small amount, but I try to tip service people every time, because I know how hard it is to work in hospitality. As I hurried about getting ready for another day of client calls, I felt happier about my busy day coming up and had a good feeling that things would go smoothly in my meetings.

When I returned to the hotel room later that afternoon, imagine my surprise when (lo and behold!) I found a note from the housekeeper.

THINK IT UP
JOT IT DOWN

COURTYARD®
Marriott.
Make room for a little fun."

MS. ANGUITA,

THANK YOU SO MUCH!!

THIS TRULY MADE MY DAY.

I APPRECIATE THE APPRECIATION.

HAVE A WONDERFUL DAY.

HOUSE KEEPING

REBECCA

f @Courtyard   @CourtyardHotels   @CourtyardHotels   @CourtyardByMarriott

courtyard.com

The note was so simple but it gave me such joy to hear from her! I felt delighted she took the time to write back to me, even taking time to look up my last name Anguita. Then it dawned on me. In the same way that writing my note to her that morning had elevated my energy for the day, I could see that my action had caused the Universe to respond in kind. My thank you note had passed along a burst of positive energy to Rebecca, which shifted the experience of *her day.*

Who knows? Perhaps she had woken up exhausted and in a low mood but she had to be at work regardless. It's quite possible that my early morning note letting her know she was appreciated made her feel happier and uplifted, and she in turn would have been more inclined to be nicer, to smile, and to send positive energy to the next person she came in contact with.

I guess instinctively I knew that *could happen*, like a domino effect. But to actually see her note, so cheerfully written in black and white, I suddenly felt that the whole thing was brought into focus. I could now *visualize* goodness flowing and good energy being passed on, and I loved it.

When I re-read Rebecca's note, I got another surge of happiness, another *whoosh*. It does work! These notes of mine elevate my energy but they also raise the vibration of the person who receives them. It reminded me of a wonderful theory proposed years ago about the wings of a butterfly. Even though they are tiny and fragile, it is said that butterfly wings are able to cause a ripple in water and in the air. The thought goes that even small ripples on the water can become magnified as they roll over the ocean becoming larger and larger waves. When those tiny ripples become waves and eventually reach across to another shore thousands of miles away, it is said that they can cause a hurricane on the other end of the ocean. Thus proving that a small, infinitesimal change can cause a much bigger change down the line.

I know not all scientists agree on the so-called "butterfly effect" but I like it and I choose to believe in it. If one tiny action of a soft and beautiful creature can ripple out to create something bigger than itself, then my project is the same: a simple handwritten note of thanks amplifies positive emotions and good will for all who touch it. And behold --- *the power of gratitude spreads,* becomes visible, tangible and wonderful!

Miracles Happening in Plain Sight

You'll recall from the introduction that it was not long into my practice of writing notes, only a few weeks really, that I began to notice that little positive *coincidences* seemed to be showing up on a daily basis. How great that I would find my missing car keys in my other jacket, just before I was ready to give up and call a cab. Another day I would hear of a road construction project just in time for me to avoid that route on my daily travels, making my drive to work far more pleasant and I would arrive easily on time. How I loved these good things that seemed to be happening with ever more regularity! But I did wonder: what *was* going on?

At first I thought it was merely strange or coincidental, but once I started calling them my *daily miracles*, a shift occurred. I realized that when you define something as a *miracle*, you elevate it, raising it up above just ordinary everyday occurrences. You are in essence defining it as something special, and by doing so, even if it's small and only personal to you, you're giving it *value*. You become present with that happy happenstance and the next day, you become excited to see what *daily miracle* might be next.

I have to tell you that once I became aware of how all this was transpiring, my life started to transform. Each day was like I was on a treasure hunt, smiling at everyone, and seeking someone who did something nice for me whom I could thank the next morning. At the same time, I was also watching for other good things to happen out of the blue because I wanted to have something fun to record as my *daily miracle* at the end of each day.

I sensed that this greater awareness that was building within me and the powerful effect of the practice must have to do with the exchange of energy, because I was sending my notes out into the world with love and gratitude, and I was getting back more in return that I ever imagined. I believe that there is energy in the intention you set and there is energy as you put your pen to paper and handwrite your note. *But could there be more to it?* Well, yes, as it turns out, *there is.*

Good Energy Attracts More Good Things

So OK, once I started my daily practice, I noticed pretty quickly that I had more of a spring in my step so-to-speak each morning, and each day was consistently producing at least one delightful event, my *daily miracle*. It was like a positive spiral whereby each day became a good day, instead of a bad day or so-so day.

Of course, I wanted to attribute all this new-found good fortune to my practice of sending thank you notes, but since I'm still a bit of a skeptic at heart, I wanted to be sure. So I started paying even closer attention to the day's events in an effort to find out if there was another pattern or cause at play. For example, was *the weather* the influencer? No, my good days were occurring whether the sun was shining or the snow was falling. Could I have hit *a lucky streak* at work? No, it wasn't that because some days still presented work challenges, be it with clients or the typical kind of office headaches. Did I have a new love in my life or a windfall of new money that was making my life so much happier and easier? No, it wasn't anything like that. So, what was the difference? Time and time again, I was led to the same conclusion: the thank you notes changed my attitude and that, somehow, made the day better.

All this reminded me of a theory I heard about years ago, when reading books by Wayne Dyer and Deepak Chopra among others, which simply stated that "like energy attracts like energy." You may have also heard this theory called the law of attraction which is a phrase that has been popularized by hundreds of self-help authors. By way of a quick summary, here's how this theory can be applied to your daily life. If you think of *your thoughts* as *energy*, then happy thoughts (or energy) in your mind will attract more happy energy or positive situations to you during your day. Or conversely, if you think only negative thoughts, you will attract more negative experiences than usual on those days.

Seeking Validation of This Rule

I'll admit that in the past, I wasn't sure I fully believed in this purported *universal theory*. It seemed too simplistic, too easy. Yet, here I was, with my little daily thank-you-note habit, and I could see first-hand that the Universe around me was *responding* positively to *my* positive attitude. Nothing else could be the reason. I was exuding a positive attitude, and I constantly came across other pleasant and helpful people, and good things just kept happening to me. I was like a magnet to all the good stuff in the world.

So indeed, I have come to accept that this well-known principle of *like-attracts-like* is true. And it certainly explains the increase in the overall number and quality of "good days" I was having; it was because I was starting out each day in such a positive and happy frame of mind. I firmly believe that the ripple effect of goodness and the miracles that I enjoy daily are things that anyone can experience. And it is a relatively easy and fun too --- just write and send a thank you note a day.

Another way to visualize how this theory works is to think about two droplets of the same liquid (such as two drops of water, or two of milk, or two of oil). As long as they are the same, these two drops will attract one another and pool together as one. But compare that to what happens if you put two different droplets side-by-side, of say water and oil. They will not attract each other but in fact repel away from each other. That's another manifestation of the universal rule that *like-attracts-like*.

So why not make this rule work for yourself? Whatever energy you give out is what comes back to you. It's sort of like the Universe is your very own hardworking, loyal-to-a-fault *butler* and whatever energy you emit through thoughts and deeds, the Universe will give that same kind of energy back to you. And given the Universe's infinite capabilities --- you could say this would be the best *butler* you could ever ask for!

Aligning Your Thoughts, Words, and Deeds

The system works, I know, but watch it. There is a catch. The Universe responds to not only what you *do* but also what you *think*, and it responds without fail to the energy you are consumed with, thinking that you want more of it. For example, the thought (or energy) of "I need this or that," will be received by your faithful butler as a command to maintain that state of *need*. My mother was a classic example.

I expect more than a few of you can relate to this next story; I know I can. My Mom was always worried about money and, sure enough, she stayed in a state of *need* all the time. Her thoughts and her actions were always dwelling on *lack*. The Universe mirrored back to her what it thought she wanted, and gave her more *lack*. Like attracted like, and her consuming thoughts of *neediness* were rewarded by the Universe with more *needy* situations.

Sure enough, this meant that whatever little windfall of money may have come her way was quickly followed by a problem on which the windfall would have to be spent. Thus my mother could just never seem to get ahead financially. I know now that what she should have been focusing on and thinking about was a feeling of *abundance* instead, because abundant thoughts would then have attracted circumstances where she would receive more *abundance* in her life.

Filled with the Goodness of Gratitude

I know only too well that changing your thinking is easier said than done. I struggled with this same problem for years, the same as my mother did, until I figured out a better way to think and act. I did a lot of reading, attended different speakers and courses, but here's what really worked for me. Once I started to operate from a position of gratitude every day, I actually began to think and act and emit energy that told the Universe that I was in possession of what I wanted, and that was *goodness,* things I was grateful for. And sure enough, I got more *goodness* back.

For example, when I was thankful for excellent service from my plumber, those pipes were fixed perfectly and never gave me another moment's worry. I replaced being *worried* with being *thankful* about virtually all aspects of my life, and now I always seem to get the best service, the best outcomes, and so many great things coming my way.

Try it and you'll be amazed how well it works. You'll see that when you show gratitude toward the clerk who serves you at the supermarket, and you're sincere, then the Universe will get the message. In its role as your ever-faithful butler, the Universe will respond by giving you more things and people and good service to be thankful for.

Since the Universe likes to read your mind and it takes literally everything you think, say and do, why not make it *crystal clear* to the world that you truly are grateful for what you have and what you've been given. Don't leave it to chance. Write your first thank you note if you haven't already done so because it is an easy way to provide excellent *tangible proof* to the Universe that you are grateful. I love this concept of providing *hard proof* because now those of you with skeptical minds who are reading along can totally get into this too.

Seeking even more proof? Is it possible that we can prove that sending and getting thank you notes actually delivers a surge of happiness to both people? Again, science has weighed in and is saying, *yes.* Thank you notes are an outward and visible act of kindness, and acts of kindness have been shown to increase the amount of serotonin in our bodies. The more serotonin we have, the better we feel. This is because serotonin is a naturally occurring chemical in our brains that helps to regulate our moods, reduce anxiety, and produce a state of calm.

I was fascinated to find that research has recently shown that both the giver and the recipient of an act of kindness experience a surge in serotonin levels and their immune systems are strengthened. So my happy feelings and Rebecca's too were quite likely boosted by a surge in serotonin, as we exchanged notes of appreciation with each other. I know I felt the joy of it, like a jolt of good energy, in both the giving and receiving in this case. It's another validation of the amazing power of gratitude.

Tips to Spread Thanks: Staying Present in the Moment

I know some days you are going to wonder why life is going so fast. It's hard when you have to rush from one thing to another to even catch your breath. But try not to lose sight of the bigger picture on those really hectic days. Stay mindful that goodness is all around you; you just have to take notice of it.

One of the best suggestions I like to share, in order to make sure that you find a person to thank daily and that you discover any hidden daily miracles in your life, is to remain *present*. By this I mean, quiet your mind and really pay attention to your surroundings as you proceed through your busy day.

If you are at the doctor's office, try to greet the nurse or receptionist by name and be kind, even if they seem to be running really late with your appointment. When you pay attention, you can maybe see what is wrong and offer some words of encouragement to them because they are likely frazzled too.

In fact any time when you are being served by anyone in a store, hotel, clinic, restaurant, or office, look them in the eye and smile. Pay attention to their desk or their demeanor, and try to connect in some way with them, by saying something pleasant if you can. It's amazing how your positive frame of mind will rub off on them, and they will be far more likely to help you out with your issue, once you connect on a personal level.

If you find yourself becoming angry with someone who is being particularly *unhelpful* try stepping back and taking a deep breath before things escalate further. If necessary, take a few breaths until you feel your level of anger begin to subside. Raising your voice seldom does any good. Remember like-attracts-like, so your angry emotions will most likely be returned to you from the other person in a loud negative barrage from them, and you'll both be in a worse state. Again the better thing to do is to try to find some kind of middle ground or common point of agreement, or at the very least, try to keep your voice at an even keel.

Personally, I like to remind myself that every person I encounter in the world is doing the best they can on any given day. Maybe they have a good reason to be in such a bad mood such as a personal upset at home or a serious health concern. Since you don't know, give them the benefit of the doubt and offer them kindness. It might be the first smile they have seen all day, and it could make all the difference. One simple smile can be an act of kindness.

Tips to Spread Thanks: Being Grateful in a Timely Manner

It is really powerful to recognize a good deed within 24 hours, powerful for you and powerful for the recipient. Anyone of any age feels honored by being personally thanked, but imagine how pleased a young person in a retail or service setting would be to get a hand-written note from a customer? I bet most young people in their teens or 20s would never had had that happen to them before, and it could change their life.

When you think about it, it may well be that they need some positive reinforcement and the company they work for may not be giving them much feedback. Plus, the worker can share your note with their friends and their manager, which raises everyone's self-esteem. You become a model to that organization that saying thank you is not a lost art; it's alive and well.

The reason I like a thank you a day, rather than just occasionally, is that it becomes a habit. And I try to make it my habit to send my thank you note within 24 hours of the kind gesture they did for me, so that they get the positive feedback and good energy boost from me as soon after the interaction as possible.

Notable Note of Thanks: Using Gratitude to Bridge a Difference

As I wrap up this chapter, let me give you an example of how I used one of my daily thank you notes as an opportunity to bridge a distance that had developed between my sister and me. We were in serious need of some positive energy and a greater level of kindness between us, and I hoped the idea of sending her a card would work. Here's what happened.

My sister and I are so different from each other that some people can't believe we're even sisters. I love her, but we don't see eye-to-eye on many things as our lives are so different. In fact, we sometimes make the joke that if we didn't have the same genetic code, we wouldn't likely be friends. But nonetheless, I couldn't imagine not having her in my life.

So that's why it was bothering me so much that we were in the middle of an argument. We kept going back and forth on the topic and we just could not seem to bridge the gap at all. When we got off the phone, I thought, *you know what?* I'm going to make her the subject of my thank you note today. What have I got to lose?

I wasn't sure how it would go because I wasn't really feeling the usual level of gratefulness or kindness. I was actually feeling kind of anxious and frustrated at first, recalling our heated argument. But I picked up my pen, with my energy and emotions still running high, and the words started flowing automatically off my pen. I thought that the note might be coming across a bit sarcastic at the start but I stuck with it.

I began with something like: "I so appreciate the fact that you took the time to give me your point of view. I know we come from different perspectives because our lives are so different, but I do appreciate the fact that we can still communicate our feelings to each other."

I continued in the best way that I could to communicate how much she meant to me because I really did want to bridge the gap. And then the most amazing thing happened. By the time I was done with my note, I realized that I understood her point of view so much better. Maybe it was because by then it had sunk in and I wasn't so angry anymore. Instead, I was viewing the situation from a place of love. *I felt full of love.*

So the thank you note, which I thought was maybe a bit ironic and sarcastic at first, turned out to actually be sincere and loving. I thought, "Wow, I was transformed into a better person, a better sister, just by putting pen to paper and expressing my feelings in the best way I knew how." And when my sister got the note, I know she felt the level of care I was trying to convey because it did serve to bring us closer together. We still don't agree on everything of course, but this example just goes to show that there are many ways that a thank you note can enrich your life and impact your relationships with those around you. Don't be scared to try something new with your daily thank you card and see where it takes you.

Chapter

5

Staying Motivated and Moving Forward

W e can all use a jolt of motivation every so often, and I got a huge boost from a new friend named Alex. I'd been telling him about this book I was writing. Alex is very spiritual and he himself had completed a manuscript and was on his way to publishing his own book so I was thrilled when he said he really liked the idea of my project. It was a great casual chat we had, and I loved his enthusiasm, but I didn't know when I would see him again.

So you can imagine my surprise when I woke up one morning a few weeks later and discovered he had sent me a most amazing email. He highlighted his experience with trying my thank you note practice. The email culminated in a powerful summary statement that captured the essence and significance of the process and it went like this.

"I started out with an inspired intention to express love and gratitude and ended up *becoming* love and gratitude," Alex wrote. "This was far more than a simple Thank You Note exercise. This is a true spiritual practice, an authentic expression of my creative self in the service of unconditional love. Perfection."

Wow! He took my breath away with his eloquence. Yes, this is a spiritual practice, I thought, not merely another gratitude exercise. And I was beyond thrilled that it resonated so clearly with an audience larger than just me. I re-read his comments and instantly any last bits of self-doubt I had were gone. With that, my book project took off again as I regained my exuberance. And I joyfully recorded my daily miracle that night and it was, "Got a fabulous email from Alex!"

This is how Alex described the process of creating a very important thank you note in his life. "The entire process, from beginning to end, was cathartic," he began. "First off, I had to purchase my own personal pack of Thank You Notes. I had never done this before, not officially anyway. I needed to drive to a store to choose the design and quantity that suited me. The product, or rather vehicle, that felt relevant and correct in the deepest way needed to present itself to me, I thought.

"I mindfully walked the aisles of my local drug store, over and over, visualizing how particular card designs would be received by my target recipient," Alex continued. "I imagined how each layout would be interpreted by the loved one I so wanted to, needed to thank for their efforts and unconditional support, many years before."

Alex felt he needed to get this right for many reasons, but mostly because he had not properly and deeply thanked this person. After all, she invested time and effort in reading the initial version of his lengthy manuscript. He did email her a quick thank you, and even told her in person, in casual conversation that he appreciated it, but he really felt this note would be quite different.

He went on to describe to me that the writing and sending of this note was a magical experience for him. "There truly is something very profound about crafting a written Thank You Note," he said. "When done correctly, when given the time and attention it truly deserves, the preparation and mailing becomes a *meditation* and the letter itself becomes a *marvelous manifestation of love.*"

It seemed so effortless the way that Alex described his emotions and the benefits of the thank you note process in broader terms. "We often hear about journal or letter writing (sent and unsent) as freeing up negative energy, encouraging the healing process," he continued to say. "This remarkable process, I was now experiencing first-hand, was far more substantial. It liberated unresolved positive energy in me, allowing me to share that energy with another in a most meaningful way.

"I most certainly did not expect this," he expressed to me, because at first he was worried that the quality of his cursive writing was poor. But as he continued to write the note, he gained confidence. "With every stroke of my pen, with every carefully crafted sentence, I could intuit a vibrational change in myself," he admitted. "I was beyond buzzing. My frequency was off the charts. My writing no longer mattered. At that point, the content took care of itself and I settled back, in flow. Empty. Full. *Free.*"

Alex even commented on the mailing of it and again used such poetic terms, I felt so happy to read his words. He described it this way: "Then came the mindful mailing process. Even at that level, there was deep emotion and a feeling of complete correctness, a final freeing up of energy. A concluding, emotional release, as my hand would physically release my little envelope down into that big, blue steel USPS box. Finally, I reflected back on the entire course of events. Then, I simply let go. Breathe in. Breathe out. A perfect conclusion to a perfect practice."

As I was reading his amazing and thoughtful account of all this, it was my turn to take a deep breath. I could hardly wait to hear what happened when the recipient got the note in the mail, completely unexpected after so many years. I was hoping Alex would tell me the ending to the story and I was not disappointed.

Sure enough, about a week later, he received a loving and grateful Instant Message from his recipient. She was gushing with appreciation. Reading his message meant so much to her, and I know he must have been thrilled to know it touched her deeply.

Yet, in his final analysis of the experience, he told me that he actually realized that the ultimate value of the practice was in the performance of it, not on knowing the final outcome. The shift for him came *in the doing. The doing and the sending.* It is magical.

Overcoming the Natural Ups and Downs

This chapter is about staying motivated and overcoming any resistance you may feel, once you are in the practice of writing a note a day. It's normal I think that sometimes any task can feel like a chore, when you have committed to doing it every single day. But for me, I have to say, I agree with Alex. The pay-back is in *the doing and sending,* and I never fail to feel uplifted once I complete my daily card.

But everyone is different, right? I didn't really experience any big pitfalls, but I learned that this exercise isn't universally easy to do. When I surveyed my circle of friends, early in the process, they all seemed very gung-ho. Their positive feedback was awesome and I even said, "Wouldn't it be great to have everyone participate and then I could do different chapters? I could have the Elena chapter, the Jennifer chapter, the Kathi chapter, and so on and so forth." They chimed in and said, "Oh, yes, that sounds great," and they started working on the project too. I was elated.

Then a few hiccups happened and a few of those early adopters dropped the practice. But the act of me asking them about their progress and hearing their reasons turned out to be a great learning experience for me. I know now this practice isn't necessarily for everyone, and that's OK. I just have to find my peeps, and I know there are a lot of peeps out there *who do get it.*

The whole thing with my friends actually became funny when it would come up at subsequent social gatherings. I got great feedback from everyone, good points and growth points, but it was my friend, Jennifer, my dearest friend, who really kept me on my toes. She said she didn't want to do it, not my way anyway. She said, "Can I text it? I don't have time. Can I just write an email?" *No, I told her firmly.*

Then the next time we chatted, she made a few more excuses and tried to wiggle around the pen-and-paper aspect of it again. We reached the stage where she said, "I quit," and I said, "No, you're fired," and we still laugh about it to this day.

I just felt so strongly about the process of handwriting these notes and posting them, that I thought I needed to really stick with that part of my vision. This is about transforming your energy, and that comes through the being present, being committed, and using the process to put your own energy in the right place, the right vibration. And that's not the same thing as shooting out a quick thank you via a text. Of course, you should always be grateful, and a text or email is better than not saying thank you at all, but in order to feel the personal transformation aspect of it, I don't think that a text message cuts it.

You have to spend the time and feel it, be there with it, and that's when your energy will shift to a higher level. And that's why I chose to share Alex's eloquent words as the opening story in this chapter. Without any particular prompting or coaching from me, *he got it.* Totally. And his getting it turned around and boosted my confidence in the process when I needed a little pick-me-up. It's all part of the miraculous timing that I seem to be blessed with through my dedication to this daily practice.

Developing Passion and Discipline

So I learned first-hand and from my friends that sticking with this practice takes discipline and passion. I have both of those in spades and I have found that three years have flown by and I am still very happy to do this daily.

My passion tells me in my heart that this practice of handwriting notes is worth bringing back to the forefront in our society. I don't care that some people call it an old-fashioned practice and that I'm now introducing it to a non-traditional set of people in this new world. It seems that most school children don't do handwriting exercises the way I did when I was in school so this is a bit foreign to them. Then there are the teenagers and young adults who dodged cursive writing in school and submitted their essays and tests online any chance they could. And we all know busy professionals who live on their devices and who can't imagine picking up a pen.

But just because the practice of handwriting thank you notes might seem quaint and out of vogue, that's no reason to discount its power to transform, that's all I'm saying. All the aspects are tactile and life-affirming; you are taking a tangible series of actions that will lift your mood and someone else's and anyone can do it. It's simple.

So what if some days you might feel tired or upset and ready to chuck the process? Actually, that's just a sign that you *need* to write and send a note that day of all days. You need to shift your energy and make a concerted effort to be more present in your daily activities. What better way than to get creative and write a little note to a deserving person?

It doesn't cost you anything to be kind, and I'm a big fan of being kind. My friends are that way too, most of the time. For example, I have a friend who was at a Starbucks once and the barista was totally out of it, getting names and orders wrong, you can picture it. Normally we would write that kind of thing off and stay quiet, but my friend was worried that day and took the time to ask the barista, "Are you okay? Is everything alright?"

And that's just it. You never really know what someone else is going through. That person who was mixing up the coffee orders or the one who cut you off in line or the guy who was terribly rude in a conversation might have just found out that his mother has cancer. You don't know what an effort it was just to make it into work, let alone put the right 7 ingredients into your coffee and get it in the right size cup.

I think it's a beautiful thing to give a person a break and because I proceed through life with good energy and hopeful expectations every day, I try to do that every time I can. It just makes sense.

Here's another example of real life where kindness was not hard to find. I had this car with 420,000 miles up until recently, so the service technicians were like my best buds. They love me, I love them, and I wrote them a thank you note at Christmastime, and I was very sincere. Then a few months later, the mechanic did something very special for me when my car had broken down and I not only sent him a handwritten thank you note, but I also included a gift card because I truly, truly appreciated his help that day.

Yet the next day, he called me and I thought he was going to say thanks for the extra gift card, but no, he said: "Elena, I just have to tell you that the gift card was absolutely unnecessary. Your handwritten note was all you needed to do – it made my day!" Yes, a lesson for me. *Words in pen, on a personal note, are powerful.* "Never underestimate the power of the written word," a friend told me a long time ago. She was right.

Overcome Resistance by Taking Action

The resistance to any practice is the resistance people are going to find. It's the resistance to exercising. It's the resistance to meditation. One of the most popular points of resistance is the always available and multi-purpose excuse: *I don't have the time.* I found that to be the biggest hurdle among my friends; either they felt they had no time for the thank you note or no time for the journal entry of the daily miracle.

To me, both these steps are significant. In the beginning they're equally significant because the journal entry is going to show you the miracle, so that's going to reinforce your resolve to write the thank you note the next day.

I must admit it drives me a little crazy when I hear the time-worn excuse: *I just don't have time.* No one actually has time until you *start making time.* When I started making time to meditate and making time to exercise, my life changed. The benefits to my body and mind far outweighed the hassle for fitting them into my crammed schedule. Now of course, I want to do those things. I've made them a regular habit. Do I exercise every day? No, I can't. But do I exercise most of the time? Yes, I do. I get tangible results and I feel far less energy when I don't do them.

Now you might ask: Do I write a thank you note every day? Yes, I do. Did I write a note on all 365 days last year? Maybe not, it was probably 363 days. But then, some days I wrote two. Some days I write three because I have so many blessings, so I'll take the time to write the three. It has become a regular practice of mine. My goal is at least one a day unless the sky is falling and so far, the sky is where it should be.

When people tell me time is their biggest obstacle, I'm not sure they are right. I think most times it's something people use as an excuse so they don't have to commit. Another way they find to dodge the commitment of it is to say: "This is hard. I don't know how to write a thank you note." Again, I'm glad to walk you through this one! By the end of this book, you will have all the ideas and motivation you need to make the time.

When I'm on this topic of resistance, I think of my friend, April. She is younger than I am, maybe by 15 years. So we're not talking about a child here, but she admitted to me, rather shyly, "Elena, I don't know how to write a thank you note." I was surprised but I am not one to stand in judgment. No one in her family ever taught her. And I think by saying she didn't know how, she was actually admitting that she was *intimidated* by it. Again the overcoming of these feelings is in the doing, which I told her.

April's excuse is similar to another popular one: the person will say she is not a good writer. Either sloppy with a pen or not knowing what to write so it flows and sounds perfect. Or they suffer with both. But who really cares? Any note you take the personal time to write and send is a beautiful thank you note.

Tips to Spread Thanks: Making Time and Making it Easy

We are creatures of habit so if you want to make this a daily habit, try to do it every day at the same time, in the same spot and have everything you need at your fingertips so you have no excuse to fall back on. Let me share some easy ways to get yourself organized and stay motivated.

Create a ritual around the practice. For me, I like to use the same desk each morning, which has lots of natural light coming in, and I keep my supplies in the first drawer under the desk. I buy stamps by the dozen and always have extra, plus I tend to know where all the mailboxes are in my neighborhood and in my usual travels. Since I travel with work, I have a small travel pouch I take with me that lives in my luggage, so I always have my thank you card supplies on hand, no matter where I am.

Here's another approach. I have a friend who likes to keep her notes and supplies in a beautiful decorative box beside her bed, on the lower shelf of her bedside table. Every day when she first wakes up, she meditates and then reaches for the pretty box.

She has stamps, extra pens, two different styles of note cards, and her cell phone is handy so she can check the street address and zip code of the company or person she wishes to reach with her card. She uses the box itself as a desk and sits up in bed to write her note. Then she automatically tucks the completed card with the stamp on it into the side pocket of her purse so she can drop it off in the box outside her office building on her way in to work.

Each night before her shower, she reaches again for the pretty box and she takes out her little diary and records her daily miracle. She may also make a quick reminder note about whom to thank the next day, if that comes to mind and she tucks everything back into the box when she's done. Or she will drop in a business card that she picked up that day of the person who will be getting her next note, the one she will write the following morning. If she doesn't know whom she will thank, she sends an intention to the Universe just before dozing off to sleep to ask that she wake up with a person in mind. This tends to work fabulously well.

Like so many people who make this a successful daily practice for themselves, they find it really helpful to have everything set up in a logical, easy and accessible way. That way, it takes less time and is a much more joyful process.

Tips to Spread Thanks: Finding Creative Ways to Say Thank You

Sometimes it is necessary to be creative in thinking of a person to send your daily note to, and I have a number of special kinds of notes that I write when I don't have a usual obvious recipient from the previous day.

One is that you can write a note to someone you might have been having a disagreement with. You saw in the last chapter that I wrote this kind of note to my sister and a few other cases at different times and I found that it is a way to diffuse the situation and clear the air. The "thank you" message itself should be written sincerely for some aspect of the friendship or for caring so much and it will work as a great thank you note.

I have written different thank you notes that I did not send because the person's whereabouts were lost to me or they had passed away. Even if the event occurred in the past and there is no way for them to get the note, the practice of writing it with love and expressing gratitude to them is still a way to validate the person in a very significant way. I like to read this kind of note out loud, so I can visualize maybe that their spirit is receiving the message in some magical way.

In another case, I did have a friend who was like Alex, who wanted to say thank you to an old friend for something very special. It was from their childhood together, and he wrote her the note, but of course could not locate her 40 years later. Still he felt that the note brought a beautiful closure to something important that had happened between them.

Then you might also consider writing an *unwritten* thank you note. It might be one that was due years ago for a gift or a gesture and you always felt bad that you never sent an actual card. Why not do it now? You can call this one "the thank you note that got away." To keep it from being awkward, don't apologize for the thank you being so late, just start the note by saying, "I thought of you today and smiled as I remembered the wonderful (gift) or (gesture) from you so many years ago..."

I'm sure you may be able to think of even more different and creative kinds of notes and as long as they involve sincerity and putting a pen to paper, it works. The main thing is not to let your practice stall because you might not have an obvious person from the previous day to thank.

Notable Note of Thanks: Renewing Connections

On March 17 of last year, I recorded a wonderful "Miracle of the Day" because I had managed to reconnect with one of my best friends whom I had lost touch with named Patricia. The reason we were able to reconnect was because I had sent her a written thank you note a few weeks previous to that.

Pat and I met in our 20s at IBM and became instant friends. Pat was in my wedding and I was in hers. When we went out as couples, we would double-date and it was the perfect match. The girls would have their own conversation, the boys would have theirs, and never the twain shall meet! We had immense fun together.

As the years went by, after I was divorced and Pat and Jak moved to North Carolina, we stayed in touch around birthdays and holidays, but I regretted that in these past few years, the cards and phone calls waned. Then at Christmas, I received a beautiful picture of Pat's family in a card and I resolved to get back in touch. I called her old phone number, which I wasn't sure she still had, and I left a message. Not hearing back, I decided to write her a thank you note.

Dear Pat,

Thank you so much for the beautiful picture of your family. I can't believe your babies are all grown up! How could it be that your children have all grown yet Jak and you haven't changed at all? What's your secret, pray tell?

I truly miss you. It's amazing how much time has passed since we spoke or saw each other. It seems like a blur, doesn't it? Not having children of my own, it's even harder to judge the passing of time, without the reminder of another human being growing up before your eyes. At least, that's my excuse.

Speaking of growing up, my niece Kelly is graduating from Duke this year and I will be traveling to NC for her graduation. I would love the chance to visit while I'm there. I sure hope we can make it happen. I so look forward to seeing you and getting caught up on all that's happening with your beautiful family!

Lots of love,
Elena

Pat got my card, texted me and we finally reconnected. We spoke on the phone that night for close to an hour, on the night that I recorded this as my wonderful daily miracle. We made plans to see each other in May which we did. She said she was so grateful that I had written the note since she seldom ever checks her home answering machine any more. As daily miracles goes, this is a great one and it all came about because of a thank you note that got away that was overdue to be sent.

Chapter

Saying Thank You in Past Tense

What if you could stop time and have one more conversation with a loved one from the past? I know many people who would give anything to do that. We can speak to them silently of course in our hearts and minds as I have done, and that is soothing. But I have reached out in another way, through my thank you practice, and it has been an even bigger solace to me, bringing me *healing and closure* in ways I could not have even imagined.

When I think about the different times that I have sent a thank you message back in time, one of the most profound experiences was when I chose to send a note to a man I had cared deeply for. His name was Harry and he was a gifted holistic doctor whom I got to know about six years ago.

This man was a complex soul who healed so many people through his practice. While I respected and loved him, it was not the easiest of relationships, and I had thought perhaps it was time for Harry and me to go our separate ways when suddenly he became seriously ill.

At first, I think we both expected he would recover so I stuck with him because I felt called to help him if I could until he would get stronger. Then we could see about the relationship after that.

Tragically, there was no cure through any kind of medicine or therapy that he tried. It was gut-wrenching for both of us as his disease progressed and it was with a heavy heart that it fell to me to be at his bedside and help him to make arrangements for end-of-life care.

That period in my life was an emotional roller coaster ride and while Harry had been a very good doctor, he was definitely not a good patient. As he became increasingly frail, he was often angry, stubborn, frustrated, and *frustrating*. After his passing, I felt such a level of residual grief, I wondered if I would ever come up for air.

Fortunately as the months passed, I began to regain my equilibrium. Then one day, I came across some notes that he had scrawled when he was gravely ill. I couldn't read them well but it seemed to be a list of care providers whom we called upon when he needed round-the-clock care, and I was still trying to work full-time.

As I held the notes in my hand, the emotions from that difficult time came rushing back with such intensity, I felt a bit light-headed. But then I thought of the many ways Harry had impacted my life, the many hats he wore. Even though he had been gone from this earth for about 2 years at that time, I decided to write him a thank you note so I could express what I wasn't able to say during the time when he was so gravely ill. It went like this.

Dear Harry:

Thank you for taking care of me in your role as my doctor. You indeed were a healer, as many would call you, and many still do. At the time we met, I thought I was healthy and strong, when beneath the surface I was actually on the brink of serious illness. You cured me of parasites, insomnia, bacteria, and taught me the value of seeking the root cause of disease rather than just stamping out a symptom.

Thank you for bringing peace to my life in your role as my partner. I always felt calm and serene in your presence. I would sleep so soundly at your house, I made the joke you turned my insomnia into narcolepsy!

Thank you, most especially, for bringing forth my higher self in your role as cancer patient. Your illness and subsequent death presented me the choice of leaving the relationship or helping you transition back home. I chose to stay.

Thank you for making it hard to fulfill the choice I made. Your stubbornness, your ill-temper, your seeming lack of gratitude ... it all provided a testing ground for my decision to stay. With stinging tears and choking sobs at times, I stayed the course when most women would've told you to "go pound sand."

So thank you, Harry, for giving me the opportunity to learn what love really means. I never thought I had it in me to do what I did for you ... to take care of you like that, to be a "wife" though we had no formal commitment, and to care *for another human being in need, without question, without conditions. That is love.*

Thank you, Harry, for being my Greatest Teacher.

Love,

Elena

When I finished writing the note, I felt a bit weird as though the room had become suddenly quiet after music had been blasting. I closed my eyes and felt at peace knowing any residual negativity from the experience of Harry's life, illness, and death had vanished. After I wrote that note, the tragic parts of those memories never came back. *All I felt was gratitude and happiness* that he had graced my life, if only for a few years. That was one of my daily miracles and it's one that continues to soothe my soul even to this day.

It's Never Too Late to Say a Thank You

Writing a thank you note to a deceased person may seem like a futile exercise but indeed it is not. I found that there are two main things at play here, and you may well experience even more than two. First, the act of writing the note is an expression of gratitude which, in and of itself, is always beneficial because it will lift your spirits.

But the second thing can come as a surprise! What can happen as a result of writing to someone who is deceased is a closure and a cleansing that is probably way overdue. We know we can't really change the past. Whatever we said or didn't say to someone, once that other person has died it's almost impossible to take our words or actions back or try to explain.

Notice that I said it's *almost impossible.* I just want to go on record saying that it is possible to change the energy around your relationship with that person and your memories of them, if you truly wish to make it happen. I am living proof it can be done. I've done it a few times now, with my mother and with Harry and a few others and each time, I felt *decidedly different* after the experience of writing them a thank you note.

My note to Harry, for example, was in reality one of *forgiveness* that I felt compelled to write. Even though he couldn't read it, I wanted him to know I forgave him for the way he treated me (and some of the other caregivers too) during the worst of his illness.

In putting pen to paper through my note to him, I was able to see *the bigger lesson* that the whole experience brought to me and understand how profoundly I was changed through the experiences of those devastating days. Once I could view Harry as *my teacher*, I was in effect *freed* of any residual resentment or ill-will that I had been carrying around. At that point, I finally fully understood the saying, "Forgiveness is a gift you give yourself." *Yes, so true.*

Spreading Thanks across Time and Space

There was another time when I recall that a single act of kindness from a stranger changed my life. I was given a reprieve that day which I never forgot and which I have since sent a thank you back in time for. I could not possibly find the person involved, but even though the note was not read by him, it was still a healing exercise for me to write it.

The note was about an event that happened when I was a teenager. I was specifically told by my mother not to take the car out late at night, but I was young and rebellious and I took it anyway. *How would Mom find out?* She was sleeping, so off I went.

While driving to my friend's house, I was listening to music, oblivious of the speed limit change from 50 mph to 35 mph, when suddenly I saw bright flashing lights in my rearview mirror. My heart stopped: "Oh my gosh, I *cannot* get a ticket!" I had no money to pay for an expensive speeding ticket and I would have to fess up to my mother who would be furious that I disobeyed her.

I got such a sick feeling in the pit of my stomach, but I quickly pulled over and watched as the police officer came up to my window and demanded to see my license and registration. As I fumbled in the glove compartment in search of the documents, I pleaded with him: "I'm so sorry, please, I can't go home with a speeding ticket!" He sternly took the documents and went back to his car for what seemed like an eternity while I sat quietly, heart beating and palms sweating, in a state of absolute dread.

He finally came back, handed me a piece of paper, and said, "Listen, young lady, I'm giving you a warning tonight. You need to ease up on the gas pedal next time!" Relief washed over me like a blanket and I felt an immense sense of gratitude for the man who had just given me a second chance.

I expect many people can recall something similar, a time when they got an unexpected reprieve that made a huge difference in their lives. My story might seem like just a small event, but it had a tremendous effect on me. I never took the car without permission again and I still find myself more mindful of the speed limit than I expect the average driver would be. And some 30 years later, I wrote a thank you note to that officer, thanking him for giving me the benefit of the doubt that night.

When you look at a past event or person, and feel gratitude after all those years for someone who may have shaped your life, it's a magnificent feeling. Who knows where I might have been if the police officer had given me a ticket rather than a warning? I was only a young driver and I might have been traumatized for a long time. My mother could have doubted my word, every time I left the house to go anywhere. I could have become an overly nervous driver and caused myself and others even more grief.

What I have learned is that the act of being grateful for these kinds of little moments brings awareness to *the bigger picture*. We are shaped by many things and helped along by many people throughout our lives. Some occupy a major role in our lives, some play a minor part. No matter the size, shape, and length of those relationships, any interaction may be significant when you look back on it with hindsight and gratitude.

A Note of Healing Years Later

Sometimes it's very hard to let go of major disappointments. Even years later, when you know you should just forget and let it go, it can be hard to do. That's what happened with my husband, Matthew. When we first met, it was love at first sight. He was strong, handsome, funny, tough, a real man's man. He would walk in the room and my heart would skip a beat.

We were so different, though. Ours was a textbook case of *opposites attract* but, unfortunately, love alone was not strong enough glue when every decision became an argument. He liked living in the country, but I loved the excitement of city life. He was shy in a crowd while I am an extrovert. He liked comfy clothes, and I liked to dress up. The list of differences went on and on.

I remember being in a restaurant with him one day, glancing at an older couple so estranged they never spoke a word during the entire meal. Instead, they ate in silence at a rectangular table, not even facing each other. I was appalled, it just seemed so sad. "Oh my God, I hope that never happens to us!" I thought, and that's when it dawned on me: *it already had.* We, too, would sit and share our meals with barely a word being spoken.

That was the moment that sounded alarm bells in my head. It hit me like a ton of bricks that day that Matthew *deserved* a woman who actually cared about the size of the fish he caught, or the camping trip he was dying to take. He deserved more than what I could give him and that's when I knew I had to make the decision to free us both so that we could continue on our own paths.

We had been together a total of 10 years when I asked him for a divorce. Our separation and the process of divorce was hard on both of us, but he remarried a few years later and now has two beautiful children with his new wife, Theresa. I believe that it turned out the way it was meant to be.

During my gratitude practice, I felt the need one day to write him a thank you note. I still felt somewhat emotional when I thought about the end of our marriage and I was tired of that unresolved pain.

Dear Matthew:

How the years have passed since that day in 1989, the day my Mom walked me up the aisle of the church to meet you, the man I would marry. How full of hope we both were, dreaming of raising children and growing old together!

And here we are all these years later . . . you, raising a lovely family with Theresa, and me nurturing a career as a single woman. I believe we're both happy — at least, I hope we are.

You were my first love and I thank you for that. And though the marriage did not last and our lives took different paths, I've never regretted the experiences we shared — even the arguments, as they, too, were part of the lessons. You will always hold a special place in my heart. Thank you for all you gave me during our time together: your love, your loyalty, your protection, your humor.

I will always be grateful for you.
Elena

I finished the thank you note and sat for a while quietly reminiscing about the fun times we shared over the years: the trip to Disney World where we rode the roller coasters until we were dizzy, and the Pictionary parties with his friends until 3:00 a.m. And who could forget the famous cookout with Matthew's "hand-picked" wild mushrooms? The next morning several friends came down with food poisoning, and Matthew insisted it had to be from *my* tortellini salad! But of course the rest of us laughed because we knew the culprit was the rather questionable mushrooms he had foraged for us the day before. Fortunately, we all survived to tell the tale.

I felt a smile form on my face as I dusted off and relived those memories one more time. Then suddenly I was aware that all I was feeling *in that moment* was gratitude for him and for his role in my life. Memories of the arguments, frustrations, and disappointments were gone. *Poof.* Just like that.

Again, I experienced how a thank you note written to the past worked its mystical and magical power. If you have unresolved emotions around a break-up or an estrangement that still haunts you, why not consider writing a note to the past? I can tell you that it works and you will feel relief.

I never mailed this particular thank you note. There was no need to send it to him. The benefit was reached. He had his own life by this time and I could see no need to stir up such ancient history. But for me, all the residual negative and sad feelings from the divorce were gone once I completed the note. They evaporated and *healed*. In this case, the healing was intended for my soul and mine alone. And it worked.

Tips to Spread Thanks: How to Create and Deliver a Note to the Past

Creating a note to someone from your distant past or to someone who has passed away might seem uncomfortable at first, but here are some ways to make it easier and more meaningful.

- You might write the note as if they were still alive and around, and you are addressing them on this earth.
- If this person is a loved one, call them by the name or nickname you used to use and include personal details or examples that would be meaningful to you and them.
- Follow your heart as to the content that you will include. No one will be reading it besides yourself, since the person has passed away or is not able to be found, so just let your most heartfelt emotions come through.
- Feel free to make this kind of thank you note longer than what can be written on a small greeting card. For example, it can be in the form of a letter or eulogy that is several pages long, if you feel you have a lot you want to say.
- When you are done, find a private moment and place where you can read the note or letter aloud and visualize their spirit hearing your words. Perhaps read it aloud to a photo of them

or as you sit at their graveside if that helps you connect with them in a closer way.

- Honor the person by putting the note inside an envelope and put the envelope in a box with other cherished letters or important papers. Or if your message is not be read by anyone else, even after your death, then set a time afterwards to destroy the card or throw it discreetly away, knowing that in just writing it, you have achieved your purpose.

Tips to Spread Thanks: Different People You Might Thank from Your Past

When you are thanking someone from your past, it opens you up to any number of people who were significant to you when you were younger. Here are just a few ideas to get you started.

- Consider that you could thank a previous neighbor who gave you your first babysitting job or hired you to do yardwork while you were still in school.
- You could thank a teacher, professor, or mentor who made a significant difference to you when you needed guidance in your career path or in your life.
- Perhaps there was a Human Resources person who went to bat for you to get you a raise or an important job recommendation that catapulted you forward in your career.
- Maybe you were a broke student or an unemployed young person, and someone made a generous gift to you that you did not expect but you have never forgotten what it meant to you.
- Think about a coach or music teacher who believed in you and your talent even when you didn't and who enriched your life by bringing out your potential while cheering you on.
- Perhaps there was someone who took you in and served as a parent figure or caretaker to you after you had left home or while you might have been travelling in another country;

imagine yourself writing this person a note about what such kindness meant to you.

Notable Note of Thanks: Memories of My Mom

In March 2016, I experienced a fabulous daily miracle that I really loved. It was on the 10th anniversary of my Mother's death, a somber day but I headed out to work all the same. I recall that the weather was gloomy and damp that morning which totally reflected my mood. When I had meditated in the morning, I focused my attention on Mom and I asked her for a sign. I don't know why I was asking her for a sign, but I did nonetheless.

The day progressed, and as I got busy with work I suddenly got a text message out of the blue from Kim who was my Reiki instructor urging me to give her a call. It was so unlike Kim to send me a message like that so I took a quick break and called her as soon as I could. When I reached her, I was so shocked by what she said. She told me that she had a dream the night before of an older woman who was deceased, who kept repeating, "Tell Elena I'm here, tell Elena I'm here."

Wow. Now that was a sign. I felt such joy to know Mom was still with me. I counted this lovely message from spirit as my daily miracle and it is still one of my very favorite ones.

Later that summer, I felt called to send a note of thanks to my mother, from one mature woman to another, so she could know that I truly appreciated the sacrifices that I realize now she must have made for the good of my sisters and me. When I read the following note out loud to her, I could visualize her listening to me and seeing in my words a kaleidoscope of brilliant colors swirling around in a joyful pattern. I had done this same kind of visualization when I read Harry's note out loud to him and each time I do this kind of practice,

I believe even more strongly that our loved ones in the world of spirit can hear us converse with them.

August 27, 2016

Dearest Mom:

I cannot tell you how much I miss you and how I would give my worldly possessions just to have another one of our Sunday brunches together ... you know, the ones that felt "obligatory" at the time.

It's been 10 years since your passing and I'm such a different woman now than the one I was back then. It is with this newfound wisdom that I express immense gratitude for all you've done in raising us three kids.

Thank you so much for hanging in there, despite the hand that was dealt you. I truly cannot imagine finding myself like you did, widowed at the age of 29, in a foreign country, with three children under the age of three. Seriously? No wonder depression and alcoholism were your companions for most of my childhood.

Thank you for exposing us to religion, though you yourself had lost faith in God. Your wisdom to give your children the choice, led me to seek my own answers about Spirituality, which in turn has changed me forever. Sure, I may have turned *into the "New Age-y" person you poked fun at, but I'm so grateful to be on this journey, nonetheless.*

But most especially, thank you for being my friend and champion every step of the way, no matter what. I still recall (and miss) talking to you about anything and everything, blunders and all, safe in the knowledge your love would never go away. Your unconditional love, like a trapeze artist's safety net, was all I needed when making tough decisions.

For all those reasons and more, I thank you, wishing someday that even a fraction of your beautiful traits will surface in me.

Love,
Elena

Chapter

Saying Thank You in Advance

Of course you most often think of a thank you note being sent *after* someone does you a good turn or something wonderful happens. But what if it were possible to send a note in *advance* of a specific event and through that note, you are able to affect the outcome of the event *itself* so it turns out in your favor, with a much more positive conclusion than was expected? *Could this be possible?* I believe that it is. I've actually written a number of thank you notes in advance that had remarkable consequences. Here is an example of one of them; you be the judge.

In April 2016, I had gone in for a routine mammogram. I really hate that test but I felt pressured by my doctor to have it done, having slacked off a few years and ignored it. The usual routine transpired: disrobe, don the lovely medical gown, saunter up to *The Machine* and brace yourself for the squeezing, hold your breath and count the seconds until it's over (one-two-three-four-five, one-two-three-four-five, holy-crap-it-hurts, one-two-three-four-five...). Finally I exhaled a long breath and was thankful it was over.

Everything went according to plan except a few days later, I received a note in the mail, indicating an abnormality with my test results along with the request for a follow-up visit which would involve a magnifying mammogram. I didn't quite panic, since I knew I was the picture of health, but I called to schedule the test knowing they wouldn't ask for it if wasn't important. To my surprise, the clinic had an immediate appointment available and off I went to get this *inconvenience* out of the way.

Again I tried to keep a positive attitude, I followed the directions of the technician to the letter, and the whole thing seemed to go fine. But the next day, I received the call from the doctor's office informing me the second test had proved inconclusive. They insisted that I should come in for a third test as soon as possible, saying this time they needed to do an ultrasound. Now I was stunned. *What the heck was going on here?* That's when I began to freak out. I went from zero to 60 in 4.2 seconds and after that, those few days of waiting for the third test seemed like an eternity.

There was no history of breast cancer in my family that I knew of. But then again, both my parents were gone by this time and I realized I really didn't know the complete medical histories of both sides of the family. It was then that my mind started to race and wouldn't stop. I started thinking the worst. Would I choose to undergo chemotherapy and suffer with horrible side effects? Or would I simply choose to let the disease progress and enjoy what little life I had left? I know it sounds silly to jump ahead to all those conclusions, but my mind went straight to my own mortality.

After all, I knew the score. I had seen people suffer and die with cancer so I was terrified. The negative *chatter* in my mind was deafening. "Sure, I am a healthy but cancer strikes healthy people every day." "I know breast cancer isn't common on my mother's side, but who knows about the Spanish side of my family?" And, of course I berated myself mercilessly because I had ignored getting a mammogram for the past few years and now it was too late.

Then the day before the third test, I had a thought: "OK, it's time for the Big Guns. Bring on the power of my thank you notes." This time I wasn't taking any chances so I wrote a thank you note in advance of the test, just to make sure. This is what I wrote.

Dear Dr. Smith:

I cannot tell you how thankful I am for the wonderful treatment provided by your staff and the personal care you showed towards my case. I am so relieved and overjoyed to celebrate the good news that I am healthy and my cancer scare is a thing of the past. Omigosh, I am thrilled to have a new lease on life!

I so appreciated the time you spent with me reviewing the test results and explaining the potential cause of my abnormality. You truly gave me an amazing gift and for that, I am immensely grateful!

Sincerely,

Elena

I finished the thank you note in advance and I felt better, considerably less freaked out about the upcoming test. I went into the clinic the next day with more confidence and far less fear than I had been experiencing in the past week. The ultrasound test was easy, much easier than the mammogram that's for sure, and the next day, I received a call from the doctor's office that everything was A-OK!

No cancer … no more worries! *Just like that!* OMG, I was OK! One hundred percent! I had nothing to fear, I was not going to die after all. I felt like I could float on air. Relief and joy swept over me like tidal waves. I had my miracle for the day and it was a big one.

I met with my doctor the next day and, sure enough he was very excited that my final test results had such a positive outcome. He was very detailed and methodical while going over the test results, just as my thank you note had described. The abnormality in the first two tests was due to breast calcifications which I was told was a very common breast condition in women, unrelated to cancer.

Had the intention in my thank you note attracted the miracle of the positive diagnosis or was it just a coincidence? I don't know with absolute scientific certainty, but I choose to believe that I was able to affect the outcome by feeling and expressing gratitude in advance.

Double the Miracles, Double the Fun!

The first time I tried to write a note in advance, I really didn't know what would happen. It was about six months before the doctor's appointment I told you about just above and I was still practicing many different nuances in the process of sending my daily thank you notes.

It was one of those days when I woke up without the faintest idea who my thank you recipient would be. Try as I might, I just couldn't come up with a person who had made my life better, easier or happier yesterday or the day before that. Plus I was preoccupied with having to hurry out the door that day because I had to do a big presentation to a client.

Then in the heat of the moment, I had this idea for the first time: What if I wrote the thank you note to Mr. McAdam, the person who organized the meeting that day, and I thanked him *in advance* of the actual event taking place? I had not done this before, written a note in advance, but I figured I had nothing to lose so I sat down and wrote a short and simple thank you note that went like this.

> Dear Mr. McAdam:
>
> Thank you for assembling such a great team of people for the meeting today. It was a pleasure presenting to an audience so engaged and attentive! I thought the meeting was very productive and I look forward to our continued conversation about a partnership between your organization and mine.
>
> Sincerely,
> Elena

I finished the note, addressed it but stopped short of mailing it. As it turned out that meeting went fantastically well. My presentation was a hit, the audience was indeed both attentive and engaged, and I walked out knowing that I would close a business agreement with that organization.

Just as I was leaving the meeting, I quickly affixed a stamp and mailed the note since I had indeed found the daily recipient. This was the first time I tried writing a note in advance, and I was amazed at how my *thank you note had come true,* word for word.

When I thought about it, it was like a light bulb turning on to illuminate the obvious. Of course the thank you notes should work in the future. The act of sending a written note out into the world serves to set *the intention,* and since that intention is further infused with the emotion of gratitude, the thank you note works double-time to attract the desired outcome.

I truly love this system because it consistently delivers double the pleasure for me too. In this case, not only was I able to secure a lucrative new business agreement, but I also got to record that success as my daily miracle. The same happened when I faced having to do all those medical tests: I ending up getting a clean bill of health and receiving a spectacular daily miracle to record. Two for one --- all because of a thank you note that was written in advance.

Is This Science or Spirituality at Work?

I'd like to take a moment and go back to the way science intersects with spirituality for a few moments because I think it will help me put this in a bigger context, something beyond just wishful thinking or coincidence. If you follow the extensive writings on quantum physics, including Einstein's view of this, you will find that many scientists maintain that our perception of time is an illusion: the past, the present and the future are actually occurring *at the very same time.*

I know this does kind of boggle the mind and I struggle myself with it sometimes but it's also thrilling that such great scientific minds are open to the fluidity of time and space. I think their theories lend credence to what I have been experiencing with regard to sending notes into the future and into the past. Under this scientific scenario and within my own experience, gratitude knows no boundaries --- it works equally well in the present moment, as it does in the past and in the future.

And yet I suspect there are still readers out there who chalk up all the good things in my examples to mere coincidence. You may be one of them. So let me entertain that skepticism for a moment too. After all, I had a good initial meeting with this prospective client and I did my homework, so I was well prepared for the presentation Mr. McAdam invited me to make. So, OK, maybe it was my diligence and my 20 years of experience doing this kind of thing that sealed the deal and it was not actually due to the thank you note that I wrote in advance.

Expressing Appreciation in Advance

I thought about this myself, so I started playing around with the concept of writing thank you notes for the future in other daily situations. I would write them each time I had a major client meeting and, every time the meeting did go according to plan, as though the thank you note itself dictated the outcome of the session, almost like the written script for a play. Then I asked myself, "Do these future notes only work in business situations, or could I try it with other situations?"

That's when I started experimenting with random events. One of the first big ones I remember was the deck project in my townhouse community. It happened last year when my neighbor Jean convinced me to serve on the homeowner's association board. I happily took on the role since I felt it was my time to serve. After all I was one of the first residents and I had lived in this townhouse community for almost 20 years.

About a year into my time as a board member, some of the decks on the units nearly collapsed and had to be replaced on an emergency basis. At the next neighborhood board meeting, the decision was made to replace all the decks to keep this emergency from happening again. I said I would spearhead the project because I wanted to help and my deck was one of the ones listed on the most critical list.

Given my natural enthusiasm, I ran with the project. I sought out quotes for the work, found a reputable contractor, did many walkthroughs, negotiated a good price, and communicated back and forth with the board at each point. This led to a unanimous vote to move forward, despite the fact that such a major undertaking would create a sizable dent into the capital reserve we had enjoyed for many years as a community.

I felt proud of myself for having tackled my assignment in record time but this was quickly squelched by an avalanche of questions and concerns raised by the rest of the residents the minute they heard the deck project would be beginning shortly. Everyone seemed to have their own opinions and worries, so when the whole thing escalated almost overnight, I decided to call a spur of the moment meeting so the residents could meet the contractor in person and have their voices heard.

The meeting was going to take place at my house and, truth be told, I was a bit apprehensive about having so many emotionally-charged people at my house. So at the last minute, I decided to pull in the big guns: I wrote a thank you note *in advance* to the most concerned member of the community. I wrote it as if it had already happened and the wording was something like this:

"Thank you so much for coming to the meeting and sharing your thoughts. Your questions and your points are very valid and I thank you for bringing them to our attention. I am happy you had a chance to meet the contractor, Gene, and get a firsthand sense of his professionalism and work ethic. Now that your questions have been answered, I am so happy that you are relieved and now looking forward to the work being completed."

As you can probably guess by now, the meeting went exactly as my thank you note had described. My neighbor did indeed have an opportunity to be heard, her points were quite valid, and she did seem satisfied with the contractor we had chosen. I was very grateful I had the chance to spend some time with her and the others, and I came to appreciate how lucky I am to be surrounded by such smart and capable neighbors who care so much. The whole deck replacement project turned out to be a win–win–win all the way around, and personally, I felt confident that it was my gratitude practice that helped smooth the way to a positive resolution.

Tips to Spread Thanks: Infuse Your Future Note with the Emotion of Gratitude

I encourage you to try sending notes to the future for things that are very important to you or that you might be worried about. The key to doing this successfully is to really visualize and feel the best result happening and to clearly give a detailed description in advance, in pen, expressing your thoughts as if the good results *have already happened.*

So the technique is to convey your gratitude in your handwritten note as if the events have unfolded exactly the way you describe it, and you say thank you as if you have already experienced it all *in that exact way.*

Try to remain upbeat and positive in your word choices and ensure that your note is written in past tense. This will seem odd at first because you'll be writing about a future event but you can always write a few draft versions while you work out the kinks and then pick the best wording for your actual thank you note.

I believe you can create your own miracles the same way I do, the same way anyone can. Why not try it and see?

Tips to Spread Thanks: Different People You Might Thank in the Future

When you are thinking about creating a thank you note for a future event or circumstance, it opens you up to a wide range of new thank you notes you can write.

In addition to medical or work situations or contentious meetings coming up, which we have already covered, here are a few other examples you might try.

- Consider that you could thank your boss and superiors for a positive performance review and outline in your thank you note what you specifically appreciated that they complimented you about. Thank them for their continued confidence in you as a strong worker and team player, or whatever is most important and valued within your workplace.
- You could thank God or the Universe for a solution to a problem that seems completely insurmountable. State in your note how well the solution worked out and how truly thankful that you are for the resolution.
- Perhaps you could send a future thank you note to your mechanic for their brilliance in diagnosing and fixing your vehicle, and you can express how thankful you are for the talented and creative approach they took in repairing your car, putting it back to fully and perfectly functioning order.
- Maybe you could send a thank you note in advance if you have to sell tickets to an important fundraiser that you are helping to organize. Make sure your note conveys your thanks and your emotions about having secured a full house at the event.

Notable Note of Thanks: Jasper The Wonder Dog

There is really no end to the situations when a thank you note will make things better. Notes for the future are even more fun because you can set out your intention in detail of exactly how you would like things to go.

This is a silly story but it's one I love to tell. It's about a woman who told me about her new dog tearing up the house every time she and her husband would go out. The dog would get into mischief and insist upon chewing up anything he could get his teeth on; this woman was distraught. She thought she would try writing a thank you note to the dog in advance, and read it to the dog with emotion and gratitude, feeling it in every cell in her body and smiling broadly at the dog in excitement while she read it to him.

She knew it was a bit crazy but she had nothing to lose. So she gave the dog a gratitude-pep-talk in the form of a thank you in advance, each time she would leave in the morning. When she got home at night, she found that each day the damage became less and less.

Imagine her thrill when she returned home one day and her full intention had come true! The dog just seemed to be far less anxious and had gotten into the habit of sleeping for the day instead of looking for trouble. Here's an example of her gratitude-pep-talk in advance. Who's to say if Jasper really took the message to heart or not, but I just love her enthusiasm anyway.

Dear Jasper the Wonder Dog,

I'm writing you a thank you note because it was such a pleasure to come home last night and not find my furniture legs chewed up or my slippers hidden somewhere in the house. Though you may still be a puppy, I just knew you were capable of better behavior than that, after all these weeks, and sure enough, you have proven me correct. I look forward to a long and loving relationship with you.

Sending you lots of doggy hugs and kisses,
Julie

Chapter

Expect the Unexpected

I have found that proceeding through each day in the present moment, grateful for all that comes my way, is a beautiful way to live. I'm not only open to finding someone to thank for that day, but I am also always on high alert for my daily miracle, which is just as much fun if not more so. The more I live in alignment and joy, the more exciting the daily miracles have become. I'm so happy to share a number of them in this chapter that have been totally unexpected and yet wonderfully life affirming.

So imagine if you will the challenge of trying to organize a customer dinner for an upcoming educational conference, like a trade show. It was being held that year in Scottsdale, Arizona, and my colleagues and I found it was like pulling teeth to pull together what should have been a simple outing. Everyone knew the whole conference would be really hectic and we simply couldn't seem to tie down the customers to commit. They all liked the idea of a gathering but it seemed to take an act of God to get it to come together, with what must have been about 1,000 emails back and forth with marketing, the various clients, and so on.

As late as the day of the event, I was still receiving various last minute cancellations and a few people on my team said, "This is crazy, Elena. Why don't we just cancel the event?" But I thought, no, it took a lot of time to plan and we had about 15 people who had agreed to attend. There was no way I was going to drop the idea then.

When my colleagues and I arrived at the restaurant, which was an upscale trendy spot in downtown Scottsdale, we were a little ahead of schedule. As we are seated at a lovely outdoor table, the waiter casually mentioned, "I hope you don't mind sitting next to some celebrities tonight."

"Ooooh, what do you mean?" I asked immediately. He explained that apparently there was a comedy event in town that same night and some of the stars, former Saturday Night Live cast members like Adam Sandler, David Spade, and Norm McDonald were all dining at the same restaurant. They had *just* called to see if the restaurant could accommodate them. I thought to myself, wow, how exciting was that? Maybe this was my daily miracle in the making! It sure was, as it turned out, but not in the way that I thought.

I gave a quick strategic look at the layout of our table and the one beside us, and I decided not to sit in the middle of our table, where the host would typically sit. Instead I chose a seat at the other end, the one closest to the table of celebrities. No brainer there.

The rest of our group arrived in the next 20 minutes ready for a great evening and sure enough, before long, the SNL entourage came trailing in, with three famous comedians among them. They sat the table beside us and we were like little kids, star-struck and acting goofy. Of course, out came the phones from our group and there were some lame efforts to snap inconspicuous "selfies" with the stars in the background. It was a bit self-serving sure, but hilarious at the same time. I was encouraged by the fact that at least we weren't bothering them for autographs. We weren't *that* uncouth.

Once the initial flurry of excitement settled down, I snuck a sideways glance at the celebrity table and, to my huge surprise, I recognized Liz Dawn. She is the founder of an organization that I just adore. Her company runs *Celebrate Your Life* conferences for people seeking self-actualization and life betterment. I had attended two of those conferences in the past so I recognized Liz' face immediately. I used to dream of what it would be like to be on stage with all those authors and experts she would gather from around the world. But what was Liz doing among that SNL crew, I wondered? I seemed to remember that her company was based in the Scottsdale area, but it seemed like an odd pairing, nonetheless.

I was so intrigued that I mentioned to my client, "Well, you may all think that Adam Sandler is the star at that table but, to me, the real celebrity is Liz Dawn," and I continued to explain who she was and why I just loved what she stood for and what she had created.

Shortly after that, Adam Sandler got up from the table and as he was walking past our table, my client shouted out, "Hey, Adam, how do *you* know Liz Dawn?" Adam stopped dead in his tracks and looked at her rather quizzically. So she repeated, as calmly as could be, "Adam, we were just wondering, how do you know Liz?"

Shocked that we would not be inquiring about him or his other high profile celebrity friends as one would expect, he stammered, "She's friends with my sister." Then my client just couldn't resist continuing the banter and she gushed to him, "Well, my friend Elena is a big fan." Adam Sandler then looked at me and said, "Would you like me to introduce you to her?" to which I exclaimed, "Yes!" as I practically jumped out of my seat.

So Adam guided me over to their table and introduced me to Liz, who was immensely flattered that I would choose to meet her among the table full of world famous comedians. We had our picture taken together – a real one, not a sideways selfie. It was really gracious of Adam and it was so much fun for my colleagues and my clients to witness this little connection.

That night was one that we all remember and love to talk about, a highlight for the whole conference that year. What started out as a truly difficult event to plan and execute turned out to be a really fun and magical experience for all of us involved, rubbing shoulders with famous people we admire. Especially for me. This was one of my most unexpected daily miracles and I know that my *Spread Thanks* practice is the reason I keep having such lovely surprises coming my way.

Learn To Expect the Unexpected

While the goodness of gratitude is, for the most part, pretty predictable, I have come to accept that no one can completely foresee what is set in motion with any given thank you note. Nor can you envision what even bigger transformations are on their way or what unusual things can happen when you practice daily thanks in this way.

A well-timed thank you note, or one inspired in a new or different way, can set off a series of events that is almost unbelievable. I live each day now fully expecting fabulous things to happen and so they do. I cherish all these unexpected joys and I really think you will experience fun things too, once you enter the flow yourself.

It makes me so happy when I find out someone new has picked up this practice and has started sending out notes of her own. It makes me smile because this practice of spreading thanks just keeps growing exponentially! I send 365 thank you notes a year just by myself and that impacts more than 350 different people each year. Sometimes I do thank individuals more than once because it just brings them and me so much joy.

Then when I started promoting this idea to others, I was so thrilled when the first nine other people joined in with the practice. Together we had the potential to impact more than 3,500 people and make them feel special to get a personalized thank you note. That is a lot of goodness to spread and from only 10 kind souls who said, "Yes, I could do that. I'll take five minutes in the morning to give thanks in this simple way, every day." It really is that easy.

Now I can't wait to tell you my other two tales of unexpected miracles! One was at a wedding and one took place on Broadway. But each one resulted from the transformation I have undergone, just through the simple practice of sending a thank you card each day.

Unexpected Grace Bestowed at a Wedding

This is the kind of story I couldn't make up or even imagine but it came to pass with such ease and grace, I still marvel at it. I know that it unfolded the way it did because I have been on my *Spread Thanks* mission now for a few years and this is an example of a joyful happenstance that I always seem to be running into.

Last year I was thrilled to be invited to a wedding. It was the marriage of the sister of one of my friends from my teenage years. My friend was named Joanna and her sister was the bride, Rachel. I had lost touch with Joanna for quite a few years, but then she had called unexpectedly. I was happy to hear her voice, but the conversation had been very strange.

She seemed so angry about her sister's upcoming wedding, dead set against it for some reason which I couldn't follow, and I couldn't seem to calm her down. A few weeks later, I heard through some friends that Joanna was not expected to attend the wedding and I thought maybe that would be for the best, given her state of mind.

As I said, I was happy to be invited but at the last minute, my date for the wedding couldn't make it. I decided to attend by myself and although I had tried to notify the bride that I was coming alone, she apparently didn't get the message. When I got there, there were still two seats assigned for me. I felt bad about the extra seat and dinner expense but I had done what I could.

It was a big surprise when Joanna walked into the reception. I thought, *what could I do?* Then I knew: I encouraged her to sit with me. She ended up being my date and I tried my best to keep her distracted. I was so happy that it worked! We actually had a great time laughing about old memories from our childhood days and getting caught up on each other's news.

For that one wonderful evening, my friend went back to being light-hearted Joanna, and the bride and her parents were so happy. Rachel had a wonderful day and her mother made a point to thank me the next day from the bottom of her heart for making sure the evening went so smoothly.

That, to me, was my miracle for the day. I could see the bigger picture and it all happened for a reason. When my date suddenly couldn't attend that was so that I could hold that extra seat for Joanna and me to sit together. I reconnected with a dear friend and was able to contribute to the peaceful flow of the event by keeping her mind off whatever she had been so upset about.

I felt so grateful. It felt like it was an "aha" moment. I never really know what to expect these days except that I know everything works out just as it is supposed to, even when there is potential for chaos brewing.

When I think about it, there were so many other ways this wedding scenario could have played out. I could have declined attending when my plus-one couldn't make it, but then I would not have been there to help keep Joanna occupied. I could have scrambled to bring another "plus-one" at the last minute so I wouldn't be alone but then I would not have had the seat to offer to my old friend.

Because I live now in the goodness of gratitude each day, it places opportunities in my lap to be a peacemaker, or a deck-maker, or a smile-maker, and I must say, I have become very good at participating in all these things. I love that my life now has this special kind of ease and flow. It is my pleasure to be of service to others and provide grace when called upon. And that is just one more unexpected benefit of sending a thank you note a day.

Tips to Spread Thanks: Looking at the Bigger Picture

I expect that by now you can now fully appreciate the immense power of gratitude, such that you can open yourself up to bigger things happening for the world in general. You are not limited to a direct cause-and effect from your daily thank you notes, but you are causing the world around you to transform in magical ways as well.

This tip is to remind you to take time to visualize and feel the emotions of a better world all the way around, one where whole countries are kinder to each other and where we are all protective of the environment and respectful of all living things. You don't need to worry about *the how* or *the why*, just feel how incredible it is to be the catalyst for such a nice ripple effect of goodness, and feel the emotional burst that comes with the greater overall transformation that is happening in society.

While you are in this expansive frame of mind, be open to miraculous events and unexpected joyous happenings close to home as well, because you just never know when your new generosity of spirit will come back to you 100-fold in a very fun way. And when that happens, why not send out a post on social media to encourage others to *spread thanks* and become a catalyst to start a world of transformation of their own?

Tips to Spread Thanks: Lack of Energy to Get Writing

So even though your world is full of goodness and light, and you've been on the path for a few months, you might still wake up one day and just not feel like writing a thank you note. You might feel: "No way, not today! It's just not in me." Then what do you do?

First and foremost, give yourself a break. Take a deep breath. It's OK. What happens if you miss your work-out one day? What happens if you fall off your diet-wagon and devour a bag of chips? *Nothing major.* It's how you treat yourself when you slip up that is important. No need to beat yourself up. You're only human.

Here's my best advice for the day you slip and are tempted to skip writing a thank you note. Do what I have done on those occasions. *I fake it.* Yes, I said that. I followed the school of thought that says, "fake-it-till-you-make-it." I remember on a few odd days, I just had zero energy and zero inspiration, so I dug into the past and recalled a special person who helped make my life a little easier.

In fact, once I remembered a very kind soul who sent me flowers when my Mom died, even though I did not know this person very well and it happened years ago. It was such a kind gesture. I couldn't even remember her last name or address, but I remembered how I felt when I saw the flowers and read the little card in her own handwriting, and that's what I wrote about in my thank you note that particular morning.

Did the thank you note get mailed? Not in this case, because I was no longer in touch with this person. But did the writing of the note have an impact? *Yes, it did.* It elevated my dismal mood that morning and gave me an excuse to get up and get on with the day. I was amazed that the shift occurred anyway, and I learned an important lesson: any amount of gratitude is better than none at all, and there is still magic in the practice even on the days you might otherwise think: *why bother?* The truth is that a thank you note is always worth it.

Notable Note of Thanks: The Hamilton Miracle

This is one of my all-time favorite stories about an unexpected fabulous outcome. I take my friend Jennifer to a Broadway show every year. It's our thing, our annual date in the city. I've grown to love this opportunity more and more with each passing year. We've seen many great shows including the revival of *Hair* and *Fences* with Denzel Washington, both of which we really loved. But, the show I'm going to tell you about here was a real coup. Jennifer was absolutely thrilled when I told her that we were going to see *Hamilton.* The creator and genius behind this play is a young man by the name of Lin-Manuel Miranda and we were giddy with anticipation, even though we had to wait more than 8 months to see the show.

Little did I know when I got these tickets for Sunday, June 26, that there would be more than a few exciting things happening that same week. In fact just a few days after I scored the two tickets for us, Jennifer got a phone call from her daughter who lives in New Jersey, announcing she was expecting a baby. Oh, joy! But the due date? July 1 of course. Dangerously close to our show!

But Jennifer never missed a beat. She told her daughter Lara, "Okay, honey, just so you know, if you go into labor the Sunday prior to your due date, I'm going to New York to see *Hamilton.* Just so we're clear." Oh my God, when Jennifer told me this, we laughed so hard!

Yet, the due date was definitely looming above us for those tense 8 months. Of course, in reality I think Jennifer would have chosen to miss the show, and I had many friends more than excited to see the performance if she couldn't make it, but I really wanted to take Jennifer because it's our special thing.

As if that wasn't enough, about three weeks before the show, I received a Facebook post inviting all my family members to my cousin Alan's surprise 80th birthday party in Nantucket and of course, of all things: the party was on the night before our *Hamilton* show. I knew that there was no way I could do both. Of course, I loved Alan, and I would do anything for him. But, this? Sorry, but after all, it was *Hamilton*.

So I texted Jennifer with this new wrinkle in our ongoing saga, and concluded with, "Guess who won't be yelling "surprise!" on June 25 in Nantucket?" And her reply was, "Well, holy cow, we better be asked to meet the cast backstage after missing the birth of my first grandchild and you missing the party of the century." We laughed until we cried and agreed that, come hell or high water, we were going to see Hamilton no matter what!

Then just about two weeks before our momentous date with destiny, I ran into my friend Kim who is a fanatic follower of all things Broadway and who was thoroughly obsessed with *Hamilton*. She assured me it was the best show in the history of theater and she asked me the date of our tickets. When I said we were going on Sunday, June 26, she exclaimed, "Lin-Manuel will not be there. He doesn't perform on Sunday matinees." *I know, right?* She totally took the wind out of my sails. Seeing my face blanch and my jaw slack, she was quick to add: "But no worries, the understudy is Javier who is also excellent." But, the damage was done. Goodness, not to see the brilliant Lin-Manuel, the creator of the musical and everybody's darling, and the man who was supposed to be leaving the show in July?

I was so devastated that I didn't have the heart to tell Jennifer. I knew she would be crushed by this news and there was nothing we could do. As the days grew closer to the show, the excitement mounted. Every time Jennifer made mention of Lin-Manuel, it was, "I washed my car for Lin-Manuel. I'm going to wear my new high heels for Lin-Manuel," and so on. Each time I shuddered a bit, bracing myself for her disappointment upon the inevitable discovery at show time.

As we walked into the theatre, Jennifer told me for the 100th time how excited she was to see Lin-Manuel. I swear, she was walking on air and I took a deep breath. We found our seats and she went to get t-shirts. I opened the playbill and sure enough, the tell-tale slip of paper fell out and I knew what that meant: they were confirming the understudies for the matinee.

But when I looked down at it, I could hardly believe my eyes. Lin-Manuel was playing and so was every single original cast member for our Sunday matinee. *How could that be?* What a miracle! I looked around, and I saw professional filming cameras throughout the theatre. As it turns out, they were taping that particular Sunday performance for a PBS-TV special that would be airing in October. So not only was Lin-Manuel and everybody else in that Sunday, but they gave the performance of their lives, the place was completely electric, it was unbelievable. And there we were, Jen and me, mesmerized by the spectacle.

I was jubilant! I thought to myself: "This was a miracle. *My daily miracle.* The miracle of the year. Full stop." But I'll tell you this, the rest of background. I hadn't told Jennifer about the usual Sunday matinee replacement for a number of reasons. One was that I didn't want to crush her, but the second was that I actually didn't want to put any energy into the thought that Lin-Manuel might not be there. So I didn't dwell on it or talk about it at all.

I was actually thinking: "Yes, chances are he won't be there, but there is a slight chance he will. There has to be at least a *chance* in this universe of infinite possibilities." And when I had been meditating early that morning, I know it's silly, but I said out loud: "Whoever's listening, it would be really awesome if Lin-Manuel were performing today." Sure enough, he did.

I couldn't help but follow up that daily miracle with a thank you note of my own, this one to Lin-Manuel. Here's what it said.

Dear Lin-Manuel:

I cannot begin to thank you for your electrifying performance on Sunday! My friend Jennifer and I are still walking on air, giddy from joy at having experienced "Hamilton."

And to think two weeks ago I was told you never perform on Sunday afternoons! I was crestfallen to hear that news, after waiting for months to see the performance. I didn't have the heart to tell Jennifer, my lifelong friend, who threatened to miss the birth of her first grandchild (due next week) if her daughter Lara went into labor on Sunday. And I think she really meant it.

What an incredible feeling of delight when we opened the playbill and saw the confirmation that you were there! My heart skipped a beat. And then we saw the cameras around the theater and learned the performance would be part of a PBS Special! Wow, now that's what I call a miracle!

The show itself was unlike anything I've ever experienced: the energy, the music, the storytelling, the dancing. Jennifer and I were blown away.

Thank you, Lin-Manuel, for the gift of an unforgettable day.

Yours with gratitude,
Elena

Chapter

The Spread Thanks Revolution

E ver since *Spread Thanks* took on its own momentum, I've found myself happier than ever before in my life. It started as a simple daily act just for myself and gradually it has become so much more than that. In the beginning days and weeks, I saw how the Universe would respond by bringing good "stuff" into my life. It was so much fun! Each day brought some kind of new-found joyful surprise: small, medium, large, and sometimes even extra-large.

Then over time, I realized it was not about the "stuff", it was about the "shift". I became a better Elena, a new and improved version of myself. I became present, mindful, kinder, and more patient. I found myself grateful for everything in my life. I fell in love with my life, all of it --- the good, the bad, the ugly, and the *mystical*.

Talk about an unexpected miracle!

Two years later, I can't imagine giving up this daily gratitude practice because it has become an essential part of the fabric of my life. I connect with people in a way I never used to. I stop and observe the smallest of transactions (while sitting with my nail technician for example or putting in my order with the coffee shop barista) and I see everyone I meet in a different light than before. We're all part of a greater picture, individual threads in a beautiful tapestry.

I feel a connection. *A genuine connection.* It is a blessing that I wish everyone in the world will eventually experience. It might seem quaint perhaps but I think that as human beings we crave this connection and we need it. It completes us. It makes us smile. It makes us feel wanted, needed, and loved. It makes us feel as if *we belong.*

Let's Return to Real Life Relationships

I find that my grateful and connected life is so rich, compared to the virtual world where so many people live today. I know that a lot of people love their online worlds and virtual communities, but I wouldn't trade my *real life connections* for any number of friends whom I might know only online. That would be way too lonely an existence for me.

In truth, I feel that technology is a necessary tool but it was never intended to serve as our entire external world. In fact, in many ways, technology is a paradox. On one hand, it connects us to an endless stream of individuals anywhere in the world, but on the other hand, it can disconnect us from face-to-face human interactions.

As a species we've never had so many *friends,* and yet been so lonely and isolated. Recent studies show addiction and mental health issues are on the rise. Many psychologists agree that the cause of such dramatic increases in these rates is actually the *lack of connection* with other people.

I'd like to make the case that if we all strived to forge closer daily connections with friends, family, neighbors, and newcomers, we could bring down the incidents of despair, isolation, depression, illness, and addiction. And what better way to do so than being grateful and being present each day?

What the *Spread Thanks* revolution has taught me is that there is a true and tangible connection that is forged by the quiet grace of a humble handwritten thank you note. In my experience, it is the best solution we have to our disconnected society. We all have access to a pen and paper, a stamp, and a mailbox. We all have five minutes on any given day that we can use to write a short thank you note.

We have within us a super power that we don't tap into nearly often enough; it's our unique penmanship. Our handwriting is the key ingredient in the secret sauce because it makes our message personalized. Each person's writing is like a fingerprint, unique to that individual. My friend Jennifer always says, "The moment I see your handwriting in my mailbox, I instantly feel happier."

And as we have discussed, the act of handwriting a note is *a kindness* that ripples out quietly into the world, uplifting all the souls it reaches. It is a little gem of joy that breaks up our stressful day, to know someone cared enough to say *thank you,* now that is truly special. It breaks through any amount of clutter, gloom, and chaos, and places in our hearts a warm feeling of authentic love.

Clicking in Step with the Universe

You know how two dancers can memorize a routine but if one of them is out of step, the routine is ruined. They will trip over each other, stumble and fall. Well, that's how I felt about my life before I started to spread thanks. I was doing everything right, leading what

I thought was a good life, and yet I was slightly out step and still searching for my purpose.

When I look back, I can see how much I have changed and it's astonishing. Here's one of the best ways I can think to explain it. You see, I used to get pretty stressed out driving to a new location for an appointment for work, especially if I was in a big city and running into heavy traffic. It would happen to me all the time. I was always worried about being in the right lane so I could get off at the correct exit from the highway. I would be barreling along trying to keep up with the flow of traffic sometimes four or five lanes deep, while trying to read the signs and sort out which exit was mine.

But for quite a while now, I always seem to find a guiding car ahead of me that is magically going toward my destination and it turns at exactly the right time to show me the way. *Coincidence?* Perhaps, but it happens no matter where I am or whatever time of day I'm on the road. It's like I manifest someone to follow almost right to my appointment.

I know that this happens because I have clicked into step with the Universe. My thank you notes have transformed my life and I am now in full step with my daily life and my bigger purpose. The Universe conspires to bring me the right people at the right time, *without fail.*

This works not only in heavy traffic but with just about everything. Whenever I felt that I needed validation about this book project for example, total strangers would magically appear at the right time to provide a pat on the back, a kind word, or an encouraging suggestion. I have also found that the right people have shown up to guide me through the book production process, confirming which direction to go next.

You can experience this kind of synchronicity by following your own daily thank you note practice. Once you are in step with the

Universe, you too will have access to this level of joy and peace, knowing that the guiding car, the encouraging words, and all the other experienced people you need on any given day will show up just when you need them.

Miracles within Misfortune

I also feel peace from knowing that adversity can be a "miracle in disguise." That peace helps me slow down my racing thoughts when something awful happens, so I can try to put it in perspective and start to look for the silver-lining.

When I think back on some of my biggest professional challenges, I remember a few dark and dismal times when I found myself having a job end abruptly through no fault of my own, and at the time, I felt devastated as if it was the end of the world. Yet when I looked back on those events just a few years after they happened, I could see that the loss of those jobs actually opened up something much more exciting and challenging for me. If I hadn't been between jobs, I would have missed out on those growth opportunities which each propelled me forward in my career and my life.

It's not just me either. I think you will see that hurts and disappointments almost always have a meaning. They are miracles just masquerading as misfortune. One of the most joyful examples I know of happened to my good friend Kathi. She was a person who wholeheartedly embraced the sending of personal thank you notes and as such she also enjoys living in a state of gratitude, peace, and being in the present moment.

Even so, no one in this world is completely carefree, and we were all quite upset when Kathi's world was turned upside down. She had a great job, but it suddenly ended because of corporate restructuring.

Kathi didn't see it coming, and she knew it could be quite hard at her age to find another position.

Fortunately, she had a unique background in interior design consulting within retail environments, and she had a positive attitude. I loved how she has always been so creative and determined, and sure enough, it turned out that the ideal match for her came up within just a few months. The new thing was something she could not have even imagined yet it fell into her lap at the right time and place, and under the perfect circumstances.

As a result, Kathi was able to take over one of the most successful privately-run boutique gift stores in our city in Pennsylvania, because the owner wanted to move on from the operation for personal reasons and was seeking an owner-manager to take on the thriving enterprise. Even the financing matters fell exactly into place. It was truly a miracle that was born out of misfortune and I could not be happier for her.

As I continue to see my own life unfolding, I realize and accept that every seemingly random experience, event, or challenge was really there to prepare me for the bigger journey. I can look back with deeper understanding on Harry's death, on my divorce, on my mother's cancer and death, and on my various financial ups and downs. They all opened me up to my inherent spiritual curiosity and zest for life. They gave me the insight to start this *Spread Thanks* revolution, and that has changed my life forever.

The Difference between Thinking and Knowing

One of the shifts that occurred within me as a result of this process has to do with *thinking* versus *knowing*. I used to like to think that all things happen for a reason but now I know for sure. There is a difference between holding ideas in your mind and only thinking about them; as long as they stay in your mind, they will remain just a pleasant idea or a theory.

But once you start living those ideas by taking action, you'll begin to feel differently about life in your heart and your soul. I call this *the knowing.* For me, taking just my small daily actions, I discovered a certainty and a confidence that I never had before, and *fear* was no longer present. Fear was replaced by joy. When I think of this, I'm reminded of my favorite quote by the late author Wayne Dyer who said: "Loving people live in a loving world. Hostile people live in a hostile world. Same world." What he was saying is that the world didn't change, *I changed.*

Here's just one more personal story that illustrates this. I used always feel that I needed to have everything perfectly planned, at work and in my personal life. I left nothing to chance because I was scared what might happen if I didn't have a firm plan. For example, I couldn't imagine going out for an evening in New York City without a dinner reservation. I would just never do that because places get packed up so quickly in Manhattan.

But just recently, a friend and I went into the city to see a Broadway show with no particular plans afterward. We took a chance, trusting that something good would transpire. We realized we might end up sharing a bagel after the show if we couldn't get a table anywhere, but there's a first time for everything and we thought just this once, we would play it by ear.

That afternoon, I was with my friend Deb, and when we sat down in the center of the row in the theater, there were two vacant seats directly beside us. As the curtain was about to go up, two women came hustling in at the last moment and inconvenienced us and half the row as they claimed their seats. As they settled in, one of them whispered an apology to me but rather than being annoyed, I smiled back and we shared a bit of a connection.

During the intermission, we introduced ourselves and learned that they were very fun women from Texas who were on a two-week tour of New York City. They'd seen just about every play in the city and had been to a different restaurant every night; their exuberance was contagious. At one point, they asked us if we had any plans for dinner after the show and we replied, "As a matter a fact, we don't." They proceeded to invite us to join them at Esca, an exclusive fine-dining restaurant that was one of our favorites but always hard to get in.

It turned out that we had the most delightful time with them over dinner, and learned that Jean had been a model, she had dated the famous golfer Arnold Palmer, and she was full of so many extraordinary stories. It was much better than anything we could have planned ourselves. It turned out that the Universe had delivered the perfect dining experience, because we trusted and had made space for it. Jean even insisted on paying for the full bill at the end of the night which was so lovely and generous. It was not hard to figure out my daily miracle that day; it was a fabulous unexpected evening with Jean and her friend.

10 Years From Now

Each day as I record my daily miracles, I am amazed that the system never fails me. There is always something unexpected and special in my experience of that day, and the act of recording it and being grateful for it just ensures the flow of goodness is never-ending.

When I think of where I would love this to be in 10 years from now, here are just a few things I hope the bigger *Spread Thanks* revolution can accomplish. I would love to see this movement impact children's literacy by bringing the art of handwriting back into focus for young school children. I believe it has the power to help them demonstrate their own practice of gratitude and forge lasting friendships and connections that will serve them throughout their lives.

I would love to reach people all over the world, in all cultures and corners, and show them how they can reshape their lives through this simple daily act of gratitude. When people practice gratefulness each day, they become thankful for all experiences in their lives, and they become more resilient, present, mindful, and loving.

In my ideal world, I would love to wake up one day and find that the expression, "Have you spread thanks today?" has become a commonplace greeting that everyone knows. You know it now and I hope you will carry it forward in your heart and in your pen, sending ripples of authentic connection and abiding love in the form of a thank you note. And may your daily miracles be never-ending.

A Notable Note of Thanks: Thanks for Spreading Thanks

Dearest Reader:

This note is to thank you for embracing your day with a newfound attitude of joy, peace, and calm. I so appreciate that you have put pen to paper through your own handwritten thank you notes. Isn't it amazing how much your life has changed and been enriched?

Through your practice of sending out a thank you note each day, you are not only spreading thanks but also spreading love.

Thank you again for helping us change the world. I knew we could do it!

With love and sincere gratitude,
Elena

Sample Thank You Notes

- The client who purchased your software product from your newly minted business.

Dear Jack:

It was such a thrill to get your order online today and I am writing to thank you so much for your confidence in my new venture. I promise I will not let you down. I know that this software will lead to the increase in sales that you have been wanting. Thanks again and don't hesitate to contact me with any questions.

Sincerely,
Jessie

- The friend or relative who stopped what he or she was doing to listen to your situation and provide support.

Dear Uncle Charlie:

Thank you for taking time out of your busy day to listen to my sob story. Just being able to air it out helped me to see that there is a way out of this mess. I already made the call you suggested and it seems to be working itself out. You always provide the right counsel and support, and I am so grateful that you're only a call away. Looking forward to seeing you over the holidays.

With love,
Your nephew Andrew

- Thanking the young neighbor living in the apartment across the hall who helped to troubleshoot and fix your computer issue.

Dear Frances:

It was so nice of you to come over last night and help me with my computer woes. I just hate when the Blue Screen of Death appears and I never know what to do. You made it seem so simple the way you tickled the keyboard like a maestro and within five minutes my email was back up. Good luck with your college exams and thank you again for being such a good neighbor to me. I got 3 emails today.

With sincere thanks,
Joe Morrison (Apt 233)

- The person conducting a job interview that you attended.

Dear Mr. Gibson:

This note is to thank you for your time today when we spoke about the job opening in the Marketing Department. I appreciated hearing more about the position at Amalgamated Inc and I feel that my skills are really a good match. If you require references or have any questions, please don't hesitate to contact me.

With thanks,
Sheila Eager

- The police officer who helped when you were stranded on the side of the road with car trouble.

Dear Officer Hampton:

Yesterday was one of the worst days of my life, when my car suddenly stalled on the interstate and would not start. I was never so happy to see your flashing lights behind me, I don't know how you knew I was there. This is my first trip through New England and you saved the day. Thank you so much for stopping and waiting with me until the tow truck arrived. I really appreciate it.

With sincerest thanks,
Mrs. Elizabeth Williams

- The friend or relative who helped get your children off the school bus when you were stuck in traffic or running late.

Dear Jessie:

Thank God you were home yesterday when Burke and Whitney were coming home on the bus. I couldn't believe the traffic jam I was in. I can't thank you enough for meeting them at 3 p.m. and making sure they were safe at your place. I know it takes a village to raise a child, and I am glad you are one of the villagers! See you Friday night at the Spread Thanks Book Club.

Hugs,
Beth

- The store clerk who helped you get a heavy purchase into your car.

Dear Michelle Mason:

I was the person who bought the microwave yesterday at noon and needed help getting it into my car. I couldn't lift the box, so I really appreciated that you saw me and came to my rescue. I know it was a busy day at the store, so thank you for going out of your way. The microwave works great. Thanks again.

Sincerely,
Tamara Boyle

- The receptionist who helped you reach the "right" person in the organization.

Dear Mrs. Wiggins:

Thank you for your help yesterday on the phone when I called looking for Mr. Kilroy. You were so kind to redirect me to the right person, Mr. Billiroye. I didn't know why he was calling but it all turned out fine. You are very good at your job, and they are lucky to have you.

Thanks again,
Josef Matus

- The administrative assistant who helped secure the appointment you needed to make with someone hard to get a meeting with.

Dear Ken:

I was delighted to have your help yesterday in securing an appointment with your purchasing manager. I had been trying to connect with him for months to no avail. I appreciated your assistance in taking my call and checking his calendar for me. I look forward to thanking you in person when I come in next Tuesday for the appointment.

With sincere gratitude,
Kelly McSpadden

- The finance clerk at the company you work for.

Dear Tonya:

Thanks so much for straightening out the tax deductions in my paycheck. Without your help in finding the error and correcting it, I would have ended up with an unexpected tax bill on April 15th. What a lifesaver you are! Your efficiency is greatly appreciated.

Your friend in the Sales Dept,
Justin Killinger

- The concierge at the hotel who secured a dinner reservation at "hot" restaurant for you to impress your client, date or spouse.

Dear Derek:

Please accept my sincere appreciation for your help with getting me a dinner reservation at Altra Volte restaurant last night. You were right: the food was delicious and the atmosphere was perfect for my business meeting. My client was impressed I got a table at the hottest restaurant in the city and I know it will help secure the sale.

I'll be back at your hotel when the contract will be signed and I look forward to another good recommendation from you.

Sincerely yours,
Greg Moore

- The housekeeper at the hotel where you just stayed.

Dear Housekeeper:

Thank you for all your hard work cleaning the room during our stay this week. I know my young children made extra work for you, using every towel and spilling their juice on the carpet. Yet, every day we returned from the amusement parks, the room was pristine and inviting. And you know the children loved the extra chocolate you left on the pillows. What a nice touch that was. You are one terrific housekeeper!

Thanks again,
April Hadley

- The teacher who spent time with your child outside of the school day to make sure he or she learned a difficult math concept.

Dear Ms. Pilch:

I can't thank you enough for helping Lou with his math the other day. He loves school but is feeling a bit shaky when it comes to Algebra, since the concepts become so abstract. My memory of math is poor, I'm sad to say, and I'd be lost without a calculator these days. Your tutoring session made all the difference and Lou feels much more comfortable solving equations now. I can already tell he is not as anxious the upcoming math quiz on Friday. The care you show for your students is obvious and I, for one, feel lucky my son has you as his teacher.

With sincere gratitude,
Becky Mancuso

- The student who went above and beyond (if you're the teacher).

Dear David:

Thank you so much for your hard work with the science project. I know you took the lead with your team members and made sure each contributed in some way to the final outcome. Bringing your team together after school every day last week made all the difference and, I must say, your leadership skills are most impressive. I look forward to the final presentation of your science project next week. This will look great on your college application. Good work!

Sincerely,
Mrs. DelVecchio

- The Good Samaritan who helped you change a tire by the side of the road.

Dear Mr. Walton:

I cannot tell you how thankful I am for your help changing my tire yesterday. I had no idea I had run over a nail with my tire so imagine my shock at seeing smoke come from the back of my car when I was driving on the highway. I thought for sure I was in big trouble! You were so kind to take time out of your morning commute to help me change the tire. And in your business suit, no less. I hope I didn't make you too late for your meeting. You should know the folks at the tire store chuckled a bit at my smoking tire story.

I'm just happy you were behind me.

Thank you again,
Lucille

- The nurse who made sure your loved one or yourself was comfortable during a hospital visit.

Dear Kim-Marie:

I cannot tell you how grateful I am for the care and concern you showed with my Aunt Connie. Although the procedure was successful, my Aunt was in a great deal of pain after the surgery. The extra pillows and blankets you gave her made her much more comfortable and she was able to get the needed rest. Your sweet nature and kind demeanor made us all feel our dearest Aunt was in excellent hands. The whole family is most appreciative.

With much gratitude,
Quigley Family

- The doctor who took special care of you (or loved one) by spending extra time to explain the medical condition, the upcoming procedure, and the follow up care.

Dear Doctor Fogley:

This note is to thank you for all the time spent with me reviewing the test results and discussing the pre-op regimen. Now that all my questions have been answered I feel much more at ease with my upcoming surgery next week. In these busy days, it is rare finding a doctor willing to spend over an hour with a patient, especially for a procedure considered minor. You truly care about your patients and it shows.

With sincere gratitude,
Marion Day

- The colleague who worked overtime to help you get your project out the door.

Dear Michael:

I still smile when I think of your kindness last week when you stayed after work to help me finish the marketing project. We got it out the door with seconds to spare but we met the deadline and I could not have done it without your help. What's even better is that you made it fun. Your sense of humor lightened the whole mood and I was pleasantly surprised at how much fun it was working after hours.

Let's have lunch next week — on me, of course.

Sincerely,

Kellie

- The massage therapist who erased your stress with magic kneading.

Dear Berniece:

Thank you so much for the excellent massage last week. I was so stressed from all my business travel these past few months and my shoulders were in agony. Yet, one hour later, thanks to your fabulous work, I was back to normal. My back, my shoulders and the rest of my body are free of pain. I feel like a new person. Your hands are magic! I promise to make massages a more regular occurrence in my busy life. And you will definitely be my therapist.

Sincerely,
Natasha

- The handyman or tradesperson who repaired something in your home recently.

Dear Irv:

Thank you so much for repairing my washing machine. I was panicked when I saw the water spill out from under it last week and fearful I would have to buy another one, which my husband and I cannot afford with our three young children. I was instantly relieved when you found the crack in the hose and replaced it at such small cost. Now it's working like a charm and I'm back to my three daily loads.

You are a true helper and I'll make sure to recommend you to my friends.

Thank you again,
Andrea

Suggested Resources

Dr. David Hawkins, Power Vs Force, The Hidden Determinants of Human Behavior, Hay House Publishing, republished in 2013.

Neale Donald Walsch, God's Message to the World, You've Got Me All Wrong, Rainbow Ridge Books, LLC, 2014.

Eckhart Tolle, A New Earth, Awakening to Your Life's Purpose, Penguin Books, 2005.

Wayne Dyer, The Power of Intention, Hay House, 2004.

Rhonda Byrne, The Secret, Beyond Worlds Publishing, 2006.

Deepak Chopra, The Seven Spiritual Laws of Success, Amber Allen Publishing and New World Library, 1994.

Dr. Joe Dispenza, Breaking the Habit of Being Yourself, How to Lose Your Mind and Create a New One, Hay House Publishing, 2012.

William Walker Atkinson, Thought Vibration, Nightingale Conant, Illinois, United States.

Acknowledgments

Bringing the *Spread Thanks* book and movement to fruition was a team project and, to my delight, each team player showed up at exactly the right time, in the perfect synchronicity I've grown to expect every day. I'd like to *Spread Thanks* to the team.

First and foremost, I'd like to thank my editor, Simone Graham, whose creative brilliance allowed my story to unfold precisely how it should have. Working with Simone was an amazing experience, one from which I learned continuously. Case in point, the old Elena would've ended that sentence with an exclamation point but the new Elena will refrain. Thank you, Simone.

I'd like to thank the other members of my team, including my branding specialist, Steve Tolerico, my strategist Stephanie Veraghen, and the photographer, Rick Banick, whose pictures captured the joy this project brings to me.

I'd like to thank the creative team at Balboa Publishing for all their help in bringing my manuscript to fruition and creating such a special book chronicling my transformation through the power of gratitude.

I'd like to thank my warm circle of friends and family who supported me throughout this project, including Jennifer Boeth, Kathi Davis, Deb Walton, Anne Bray, Mary McSpadden, Anella and Craig Wetter,

April and Chris Hadley, my sisters Margarita and Barb, my cousins Rosemary and Eileen, my nieces and nephews Michelle, Derek, Kelly, Mary and David. Your love and support is invaluable to me and I treasure all of you.

About the Author

E lena Anguita is a change agent, author, and speaker who passionately supports education, literacy, and helping people learn. In 2017, she launched the *Spread Thanks* revolution, a movement to encourage personal gratefulness through the sending of daily thank you notes. Her enthusiasm and professionalism are putting this simple, yet transformational practice on the map as more and more people are creating miracles in their lives through gratitude.

In her corporate career, Elena is an account executive for a leading American educational products company. She works closely with K-12 schools providing solutions to help educators become more productive and to help school children succeed. This career path began more than 18 years ago where Elena excelled within IBM's Educational Systems Division. Over the years, Elena has been nationally recognized with multiple awards, both for sales achievement and customer satisfaction, including the prestigious IBM Golden Circles which are granted only to the company's highest achievers. Elena lives in Pennsylvania and has a gift for connecting people and ideas in miraculous ways.

CPSIA information can be obtained
at www.ICGtesting.com
Printed in the USA
BVOW08s2309101117
499972BV00001B/1/P

9 781504 388818